Series / Number 02-029

Power, Balance of Power, and Status in Nineteenth Century International Relations

RICHARD ROSECRANCE
Cornell University

ALAN ALEXANDROFF
Cornell University

BRIAN HEALY
University of Pennsylvania

ARTHUR STEIN
Yale University

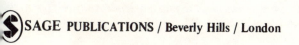

SAGE PUBLICATIONS / Beverly Hills / London

For information address:

SAGE PUBLICATIONS, INC.
275 South Beverly Drive
Beverly Hills, California 90212

SAGE PUBLICATIONS LTD
St George's House / 44 Hatton Garden
London EC1N 8ER

International Standard Book Number 0-8039-0475-4

Library of Congress Catalog Card No. 74-83124

FIRST PRINTING

When citing a professional paper, please use the proper form. Remember to cite the
correct Sage Professional Paper series title and include the paper number. One of the
two following formats can be adapted (depending on the style manual used):

(1) AZAR, E. E. (1972) "International Events Interaction Analysis." Sage Professional Papers in International Studies, 1, 02-001. Beverly Hills and London: Sage
Pubns.

OR

(2) Azar, Edward E. 1972. *International Events Interaction Analysis.* Sage Professional Papers in International Studies, Vol. 1., no. 02-001. Beverly Hills and London:
Sage Publications.

CONTENTS

Power, Balance of Power, and Status in Nineteenth Century International Relations

RICHARD ROSECRANCE
Cornell University

BRIAN HEALY
University of Pennsylvania

ALAN ALEXANDROFF
Cornell University

ARTHUR STEIN
Yale University

INTRODUCTION

It is a commonplace that "power," "balance of power" and "status" have impact in social relationships. Individuals with greater "power" will have influence upon those with less (Lasswell and Kaplan, 1950). Persons with higher "status" will be treated differently from those with lower social standing (Tedeschi, 1972). Among social groups competing for influence, certainly among states, it is a traditional contention that an approximation toward balance of power will emerge (Hinsley, 1962). If it does not, higher levels of conflict are deemed likely (Gulick, 1955).

What is striking in any survey of the literature on these topics, however, is how much disagreement there is among social scientists. Is "power" an attribute in that each social actor has an absolute stock of it (Knorr, 1956); or is it to be defined relationally (Lasswell and Kaplan, 1950), so that one actor's position carries weight only in relation to the position of others? Is the acquisition of a large amount of power (defined either absolutely or relatively) by an actor desirable in terms of the impact upon the larger social system? Or will such an agglomeration of power in a single

AUTHORS' NOTE: *The authors would like to express their thanks and indebtedness to Professors Edward Azar, Maurice East, Harry Eckstein, Jeffrey Hart and Samuel Williamson and to Mr. David Korn for help or suggestions in the preparation of this paper. Mrs. Barbara Stephens typed innumerable drafts and the final version.*

hand promote conflict with other actors? Regardless of the answer to these two questions, students are not certain whether it is the power of the individual actor or only of his social group (coalition) which matters. Is it true that even if a single actor has a large amount of power (or status) the regard in which he is held by others is largely determined by the total power (or status) of the group to which he belongs?

There is an extensive literature in domestic political analysis on this topic (Dahl, 1957, 1968; Lasswell and Kaplan, 1950; March, 1955, 1956, 1957; Simon, 1953; Riker, 1964; Faley and Tedeschi, 1971). In the field of international relations, the situation is if anything even more chaotic. Respectable historical investigators have disagreed whether it is better to have a balance of power in the international system or to have an overbalance in the hands of a preponderant coalition (Taylor, 1954; Langer, 1950). Political scientists have differed over the same issue (Doran, 1971; Organski, 1968a, 1968b). There is uncertainty whether the critical condition is the power of a single state or of the alliance of which it is a part (Hinsley, 1962; Organski, 1968b).

In regard to "status" it is not clear that the nations at the top of the international social pyramid are also those which elicit the greatest amount of cooperation from others (Singer and Small, 1966a). Honorifics may not confer realistic benefits. The relationship between "status" and "power" is also uncertain. A venerable strand of analysis contends that it is the disparity between the power of an actor and his status which leads to conflict. In international relations this effect might be most typically seen where the power of one nation exceeds the amount of status accorded to it, while the power of another is less than its status or prestige. The first then is expected to contend with the second to gain a greater share of the prestige benefits. Galtung calls this phenomenon "rank disequilibrium" and an entire literature has grown up on this subject alone (Galtung, 1964, 1966a, 1966b; Gleditsch, 1969; East, 1969, 1970, 1972; Wallace, 1970; Singer et al., 1972). It remains unclear in systemic analyses, however, whether the nations suffering the greatest disparity between power and status are those which are also the most engaged in international conflict (Ray, 1974).

A major reason for the great differences in viewpoint on these concepts and relationships is that (at least until recently) few attempts have been made to operationalize "power" and "status" or to measure the amount of conflict in the system or between two actors. Both "power" and "status" are protean terms, capable of reinterpretation and extension in different linguistic contexts. "Power" is particularly difficult to grasp concretely because statesmen operate on "perceived" notions of power which may or may not be accurate. For different periods of time, it is certainly clear that

American and Soviet power was underestimated; the power of Britain and France overestimated. Decisions were taken utilizing these erroneous estimates which had great impact in the system. Attempts at more accurate rendering of power relationships neglect the perceptual dimension and thus do not fully account for national decisions.

It remains true, however, that most "power" and "status" theories of international politics have been stated in objective form. It is the objective power or the objective status of an actor which is supposed to determine the behavior of other actors, and to condition their attitude toward him. If it could be shown that such objective factors did not actually determine such behavior or attitude, a classical strand of international theorizing would be refuted. It is therefore important to find a basis for assessing such theories to see whether the inconsistency of previous findings can be remedied, or, if not, to narrow the range of divergence among approaches. It simply cannot be the case that a "balance of power" is both a restraint on international conflict and a stimulus to it: that rank disequilibrium is both associated and not associated with hostility between states. Somewhere errors in fact or definition have been made. The present essay is an effort at redefinition of the critical theories and a reassessment of their empirical validity.

OBJECTIVES OF THIS ESSAY

Specifically the objectives of this essay are five-fold:

(1) to formulate as clearly as possible different clusters of "power," "balance of power" and "status" theories of international behavior so that they may be subjected to appropriate test;

(2) to develop valid approximations to or measures of "power," "status," "balance of power" which permit the operationalization of the different clusters of theory;

(3) to formulate valid measures of international "cooperation and conflict" so that the measures of "power" and "status" may be compared with the resulting degree of "cooperation" and "conflict" both as between two nations and within the system as a whole;

(4) to seek to establish a relationship among "power," "balance of power," "status" and the dependent variables of "cooperation" and "conflict," thereby testing the theories sketched in (1); and

(5) to draw conclusions about the general applicability of such theories in the nineteenth century, with comments upon the results of such an investigation for twentieth century practice.

Each of these tasks will be attacked in the succeeding sections of this paper.

CLUSTERS OF THEORY

Enough has been said above to indicate the range of competing theories and approaches in the international relations field. What is necessary now is to delineate the separate "clusters" or "islands" of theory that are deserving of empirical test. Roughly speaking, there appear to be five such clusters. First, there are a series of propositions or assertions which link conflict and cooperation, peace and war in the system to the absolute amount of some crucial quantity: "power," "status" or other. States with the high stocks of this quantity could then be expected either to enjoy high levels of cooperation, or to be the objects of great rivalry or conflict.

A second cluster would relate cooperation and conflict to relative amounts of the crucial quantity (power, status or other) possessed by states. Unlike absolute measures, the cooperation derived by states on relative bases, would depend strictly upon their rank in the hierarchy of the value possessed.[1]

A third cluster of theories would relate the amount of cooperation and conflict derived to the change in the amount of power or status (Singer et al., 1972). It might be true that the amounts of power or status possessed (whether measured absolutely or relatively) by actors would be strictly irrelevant to the amount of cooperation they receive, while the change in power or status would be more directly related to cooperation gained. According to some historical hypotheses, German power may not have been preeminent during the Bismarckian system but the change in the German position was so dramatic that Berlin gained the greatest share of European cooperation.

A fourth series of theories links disparity between power and status and the amount of cooperation received or given. Is there a relationship between conflict and the amount of discrepancy between power and status in the international system? If this pattern does not hold overall, is there a relationship between conflict and negative discrepancies (that is, where power exceeds status)? This hypothesis should be tested separately because it is plausible that nations with high power but low status might be prone to initiate conflict while those with high status and low power would not be so prone.

Finally, it is possible that there is no relationship between power and status (measured absolutely, or relatively), change in power or status, status discrepancy (or rank disequilibrium) and cooperation. An alternative hypothesis would be that it is the way in which power or status is exercised, and not their amount that is a crucial determinant of the amount of cooperation in the system. If there were some appropriate way of measuring the *exercise* of power, this variable might turn out to be a more sensitive predictor of cooperation and conflict than gross measures or comparisons of the amount of power or status.

In what period of historical reality should these theories be tested? If theory is to have the greatest contemporary relevance a strong case can be made for the present or immediate past period. Extrapolations to the future, could then most easily be made. The difficulty with such a solution, however, is that the data for such a test are not fully available. While the general patterns of cooperation and conflict in the international system can be seen, specific dyadic relationships and even some major events are partly obscured by the barrier of official secrecy. Until the diplomatic collections and archives become available, historians will not be able to observe the full record of relations among states. Lacking the diplomatic historical materials one, of course, could use newspaper sources as a surrogate. The special complication of newspaper sources, however, may be that they tend to overstress conflictual events and thus to miss the underlying substratum of cooperation that lies beneath the surface. Conflict tends to appear more characteristic than in fact it is.[2] In any event, sources which fail to capture the complete diplomatic record are unsatisfactory.

The problem of sources then, augurs in favor of testing power generalizations in a period in which the diplomatic material is fully available. For most European powers this means prior to World War I. A choice in favor of the Bismarckian or post-Bismarckian periods, however, raises the question of relevance: in what sense could it be argued that relationships in the eighteen seventies or eighties could have application to the world of today? There are a number of answers to this question. First, the problem of state relationships has structurally not changed since the French Revolution when the nation-state first took form. Since 1790 states have been in process of becoming instruments of their nationalized publics. In structural terms factors which helped to account for the accommodation of interests and the limitation of conflict in the nineteenth century should have application today.

Second and more fundamentally, in basic respects human behavior must be similar across historical epochs. If human nature does not change, there must be some behavioral constants. The problem then becomes that of searching out elements of commonality. These elements can be found as long as comparisons are generic rather than specific. The greater the historical distance between behavior to be compared, the more generalized and aggregative must be the principles of comparison. The same is of course true of comparisons of different social and political institutions in different geographic locations in a given historical epoch. The more universal the political behavior one wants to describe and analyze, the less system-specific must the terminology be. Thus the typical traditional political categories used in the analysis of Western democratic government (such as "executive, legislative and judicial," "political parties," "interest groups" and so on) could not be used in the analysis of non-Western societies and politics. More general terminology (such as "rule-making," "interest articulation," "interest aggregation" and the like) had to be employed to compare political systems across geographic and developmental lines. Thus, there is no difficulty in principle in making cross-temporal comparisons or in relating the behavior of the nineteenth century diplomatic system to the twentieth century political system. The difficulty is practical: on what conceptual bases to make the linkage.

This introduces a third and very particular reason for the choice of nineteenth century diplomacy as the setting in which to test the variety of power and status theories. The nineteenth century, and particularly the decade of the eighteen seventies, has been regarded as the archetype of the balance of power system. If power variables were ever to have influence in world politics, they should be observed in operation in the eighteen seventies.

Indeed, power variables should have even greater application in the Bismarckian system of international relations than they do today. Today, we are told, military power is unusable or at a discount (Knorr, 1966). Thus, for those exponents of the various theories involved, the choice of the eighteen seventies is one most favorable to the demonstration of power and balance of power hypotheses.

Finally there is an especial contemporary relevance to a survey of the diplomacy of the eighteen seventies. While strict power factors may have changed in the interim, the shifting alignments of the Bismarckian period may have even greater application to the world of the nineteen eighties than do contemporary cold war alliances. The diplomacy of five major units: Russia, America, W. Europe, China and Japan may be more akin to the diplomacy of the eighteen seventies than to recent bipolarity.

For all these reasons we have chosen to center the testing of power, status, and balance of power theories in the decade of the eighteen seventies. Diplomats, historians and even statesmen from the era concerned talked incessantly about power. Does it follow that power and status are variables which help to explain a large part of international behavior?

APPROXIMATIONS TO "POWER," "STATUS," AND "BALANCE OF POWER"

In order to test such claims, it is necessary to have a satisfactory measure of "power"; "balance of power"; and "status." These are extremely difficult and evanescent terms; indeed in a strict sense, they are capable of unlimited extension and are hence undefinable (Rosecrance, 1961). It is impossible to tell how to combine "zeal" with "military strength" in reaching a reliable compound of "power." Indeed, even if this could be done so that x units of "zeal" could be regarded to offset y units of "military strength," the equation could not be written because "zeal" cannot be estimated concretely. The same is true of other elements that are typically regarded to form part of a nation's "power": "quality of government"; "quality of diplomacy"; "morale" and so on (Morgenthau, 1973). The difficulty of measuring "power" in this comprehensive sense would be critical if the theories to be tested were formulated in such terms. If they were formulated in such terms, however, *they could not be tested at all* since "power" could not be defined or precisely approximated. We do not propose to attempt to assess such grandiose formulations: rather, we seek to find approximations to the *objective* power of a state, the power which is capable of objective assessment. Further, as noted above, it is crucial to separate the amount of power from its modes of exercise if the two different competing explanations are to be compared. If terms like "quality of diplomacy," "quality of government" and so on are to be included in "power," then the means of exercise of power becomes identical with power itself and no assessment of the respective utilities of the two different approaches is possible.

It follows then that what is necessary for an objective approximation to or measurement of "power" is data on a nation's objective qualities: such factors as economic strength and potential, military preparedness, degree of modernization, demographic strength, and financial liquidity and stability. We have gathered just such data for the five major European powers in the period, 1870-1881. In all, some 107 different variable measures have been compiled on a yearly basis (see Table 1). These measures are balanced between somewhat crude military and demographic variables (reflecting the sheer ponderousness or "weight" of a nation) and financial, educational, economic, and communicational variables (that indicate the degree of modernization, the speed and flexibility with which "weight" may be exercised). In addition, twenty-five variables were chosen for inclusion in a "power index": this index included those measures from each crucial category which seemed best to "represent" the category in question.[3] Seven categories were included in the index: demographic, economic, military, educational-scientific, financial, trading and fiscal. Nations which

Table 1. Approximations of Power and Status

Demographic Variables
  Population
  Population Density
  Urban Population (over 50,000)
  Emigrants
Education Variables
  Primary School Enrollment
  Primary School Enrollment/Capita
  Secondary School Enrollment
  Secondary School Enrollment/Capita
  Primary and Secondary Enrollment
  Primary and Secondary Enrollment/Capita
  University Enrollment
  University Enrollment/Capita
  Total School Enrollment
  Total School Enrollment/Capita
Financial Variables
  Amount Coinage Minted Annually
  Wheat Price
  Bank Discount Rate
  Open Market Discount Rate
  Number of Bonds
  Total Amount of Bonds Unredeemed
    on London Market
  Average Market Price of Bonds
    (Par = 100)
  Cost of Living
  Gross Money Wages
  Discount Rate--Yearly Spread
  Number of Changes in Discount Rate
Fiscal Variables
  Total Government Expenditures
  Total Revenue
  Military Expenditure
  Interest on Debt
  % Military of Total Expenditures
  % Interest of Total Expenditures
  Total Public Debt
  Surplus or Deficit--Government
    Revenues and Expenditures
Military Variables
  Military Expenditure
  % Military of Total Expenditures
  Naval Tonnage
  Number of Ironclads
  Men in Army
Transactional Variables
  Telegrams
  Telegrams/Capita
  First Class Mail
  First Class Mail/Capita
  All Mail
  All Mail/Capita
Economic Power Variables
  Pig Iron Production
  Steel Production
  Coal Production
  Railroad Mileage
  Railroad Mileage/Square Mile
  Telegraph Mileage
  Telegraph Mileage/Square Mile

Diplomatic Variables
  Number of Diplomatic Recognitions
  Foreign Diplomats in Austria
  Foreign Consuls in Austria
  Foreign Diplomatic Representatives in Austria
  Foreign Diplomats in England
  Foreign Consuls in England
  Foreign Diplomatic Representatives in England
  Foreign Diplomats in France
  Foreign Consuls in France
  Foreign Diplomatic Representatives in France
  Foreign Diplomats in Germany
  Foreign Consuls in Germany
  Foreign Diplomatic Representatives in Germany
  Foreign Diplomats in Russia
  Foreign Consuls in Russia
  Foreign Diplomatic Representatives in Russia
Trade Variables
  Imports General[a]
  Exports General
  Imports Special[b]
  Exports Special
  Imports Totals
  Exports Totals
  Imports Bullion General
  Exports Bullion General
  Imports Bullion Special
  Exports Bullion Special
  Surplus or Deficit--General Commerce
  Surplus or Deficit--Special Commerce
  Surplus or Deficit--Bullion General
  Surplus or Deficit--Bullion Special
  Imports from Austria
  Exports to Austria
  Imports from England
  Exports to England
  Imports from France
  Exports to France
  Imports from Germany
  Exports to Germany
  Imports from Russia
  Exports to Russia
  Relative Acceptance Imports from Austria
  Relative Acceptance Exports to Austria
  Relative Acceptance Imports from England
  Relative Acceptance Exports to England
  Relative Acceptance Imports from France
  Relative Acceptance Exports to France
  Relative Acceptance Imports from Germany
  Relative Acceptance Exports to Germany
  Relative Acceptance Imports from Russia
  Relative Acceptance Exports to Russia
  Surplus or Deficit--Trade with Austria
  Surplus or Deficit--Trade with England
  Surplus or Deficit--Trade with France
  Surplus or Deficit--Trade with Germany
  Surplus or Deficit--Trade with Russia
  Surplus or Deficit--Trade with Major Powers

[a]General: Trade including reexport
[b]Special: Trade excluding reexport

did not have a very large demographic base might yet be superior on indices of economic or educational development. Nations which were not strong militarily might have great potential in terms of high modernization, fiscal stability, and trading position. (See Table 2.) In the absence of explanatory theory which would provide a basis for weighting these variables in the compilation of an index, we assume that each variable has equal status. At least for the eighteen seventies, such a procedure is intuitively satisfying in that it places France and England in the lead at the beginning of the decade, both of them giving place to Germany at the end. Russia and Austria-Hungary remain a distant fourth and fifth respectively.

If such an index validly represents objective power assessments for the eighteen seventies, "balance of power" becomes easy to measure. If coalitions contain states which sum to an approximate balance in strength, then there is a "balance of power." If one coalition contains the strongest states and another the weaker states, then power certainly is not balanced.

More difficult is the measurement of "status." While "power" has obvious objective referents, "status" does not. Insofar as status is equivalent to reputation, it might be measured by obtaining the views of national leaders about their and other states' standing. This has not been and could not be done. Diplomats do not provide such estimates; nor, if they did,

Table 2. Twenty-Five Power Variables

Military

Military Expenditure
Percent of Budget Spent on Military
Number of Military Personnel
Number of Ironclad Warships

Demographic

Population
Urban Population

Fiscal

Total Government Expenditure
Total Government Revenue
Surplus or Deficit in
  Government Budget

Trade

Surplus or Deficit with the
  Major Powers

Economic

Pig Iron Production
Steel Production
Coal Production
Telegraph Mileage
Telegraph Mileage/Capita
Railroad Mileage
Railroad Mileage/Capita

Educational

Primary School Enrollment
Primary School Enrollment/Capita
University Enrollment
University Enrollment/Capita

Financial

Bank Discount Rate[a]
Open Market Discount Rate[a]
Discount Rate--Yearly Spread[a]
Number of Changes in Discount Rate[a]

a. While it was assumed that a nation's power would vary positively with the other variables, bank discount rate and open market discount rate were related to power inversely: that is, it was assumed that a low rate of discount would indicate a plenitude of financial resources and therefore greater power. Also, the larger the spread in the rate of discount (the greater the instability and fluctuations) the lower the presumed power. For similar reasons, the greater the number of changes in the discount rate, the lower the power.

could they be relied upon or a diplomat's calling would be misnamed. A partial surrogate for status might be found in the number of diplomatic recognitions accorded to a state by other powers (Singer and Small, 1966a; Wallace, 1970). Another measure, still not fully satisfactory, would be the number of diplomats accredited to a foreign capital, with the assumption that the more diplomats accredited, the higher the status (Brams, 1966). As East (1972) has argued, "the general theory underlying this indicator of prestige closely parallels that of the reputational school of social position." Yet, neither of these measures is adequate in itself. Failing other objective measures, we have chosen to use both as indicators of status. The reader should be aware of our caveats, however, and that we are continuing to search for better measures of national status and prestige.

MEASURES OF INTERNATIONAL COOPERATION AND CONFLICT

If power, balance of power and status theories are to be tested, they must be compared both dyadically and systemically to a valid and reliable indicator of the amount of international cooperation and conflict. At least four possible sources of cooperation and conflict data might be used for the eighteen seventies. The first, similar to the data used in the contemporary period by many analysts, is newspaper data. Newpapers, however, do not have access to secret diplomacy; many of the events which they record are trivial; and there is also the possibility of systematic bias. A second source might be data on wars (as evidence of conflict) and alliances (as evidence of cooperation). Singer and his associates have plumbed this material with great profit (Singer and Small, 1968). Alliances and wars, however, represent only the endpoints of the continuum of cooperation and conflict. The vast middle segment of this continuum (which represents less conflict than war and less cooperation than alliance) is left out. Since the vast preponderance of international actions fall within this category, this is a crucial disadvantage. A third approach might be to utilize archival material or the official collections of documents issued by national foreign offices. The difficulty here is winnowing the grain from the chaff: most of what transpires between governments is of little importance; most of the actions taken pass beneath the threshold of diplomatic significance. For example, an American Secretary of State sees and takes action upon only about .1 to .3% of the incoming cable traffic per day (Goodman et al., 1974). The question is then posed: how might the important actions and events be screened from the unimportant? A fourth method, and the one employed here, is to use the guidance of the diplomatic historian. On the basis of his expert knowledge he is able to distinguish between significant and trivial occurrences. Presumably, those acts and events which diplomatic historians have seen fit to record in their works are those that the most highly trained and knowledgeable scholars regard as most important and most relevant to an understanding of the period concerned. But how are their works to be used? How might one construct some measure of international cooperation and conflict from the salient diplomatic historical surveys? First, it is necessary to develop a list of standard sources. In our case we have used works on the American Historical Association's *Guide to Historical Literature* (1961). In addition we have further limited this list by requiring in addition that the works in question cover at least a twelve-year historical period. The specification of a twelve-year rule prevents inclusion of essentially monographic treatments of short time periods. We also rule out studies that deal solely with a functional area of interest (such as colonial or naval policy). The reason for requiring generality of treatment is that inclusion of purely mono-graphic and specialized treatments would alter criteria of significance. The general diplomatic historians aim at a roughly common level of abstraction and a roughly similar standard of significance. To have included mono-graphic accounts of, say, the Near Eastern Crisis (1875-78) or the negotia-tion of the Dual Alliance (1878-79) would have skewed the list toward two specific episodes; it would not have provided relatively "even" cover-age of the entire period. Moreover, since detailed treatments do not exist for each microscopic time period in the monographic literature, there was no way to include all the monographic accounts and still attain an evenness of abstraction and a common standard of significance.

The sources used were works by: Albertini, Fay, Hinsley, Langer, Schmitt, Sontag, and Taylor. Other sources might also have been em-ployed, but the marginal utility of plumbing additional sources is already very small in that each new source adds less and less to the previously formulated list of events. The procedure used to "code" these sources was as follows:

1. Each coder (historians and political scientists) was given instructions specifying what an event is and how to code it (see Goodman et al., 1974).

2. Coders were instructed to list each event recorded by the historian in language as close as possible to that of the historian.

An initial check on the reliability of event selection was made. In numerous trials coders selected events from the same passage in several different sources. The average overlap of events was over 85%—that is, less than 15% of the events listed by any given coder were not listed by other coders. Moreover, reliability improved in later stages of the project. After cross-coder reliability checks, each coder went on to code all events for the

Table 3.
Measures of Cooperation and Conflict

1. Cooperation/conflict scores for a nation as actor on the international system.
2. Cooperation/conflict scores for a nation as actor on the major power subsystem.
3-7. Cooperation/conflict scores for a nation as actor on England, France, Germany, Austria-Hungary, Russia—separately.
8. Cooperation/conflict scores for a nation as target of the international system.
9. cooperation/conflict scores for a nation as target of the major power subsystem.
10-14. Cooperation/conflict scores for a nation as target of England, France, Germany, Austria-Hungary, Russia—separately.
15. The number of events in which a nation was the initiator of actors on the international system.
16. The number of events in which a nation was the initiator of actions on the major power subsystem.
17-21. The number of events in which a nation was the initiator of actions on England, France, Germany, Austria-Hungary, and Russia—separately.
22. The number of events in which a nation was the target of actions by the international system.
23. The number of events in which a nation was the target of actions by the major power subsystem.
24-28. The number of events in which a nation was the target of actions by England, France, Germany, Austria-Hungary, and Russia—separately.
29. Systemic balance of cooperation (cooperation received from the international system minus cooperation given to the international system). o
30. Major power balance of cooperation (cooperation received from the major powers minus cooperation given to the major powers).

required period in one historical source. Events were coded in the order in which they appeared in the text. The collation of the event lists of separate historians resulted in the compilation of a single master list of events for the 1870-1881 period.

After the creation of a cooperation-conflict scale (see Goodman et al., 1974) the master list was formally scaled with interscaler reliabilities over .90. Each dyadic interaction among states received a specific scale score. This made possible the testing of hypotheses concerning the amounts of cooperation or conflict between two states as well as those dealing entirely with systemic cooperation. In this paper the measures of international cooperation-conflict were used in more than thirty different forms, each dealing with the major nations—England, France, Germany, Austria-Hungary and Russia—year-by-year. It thus became possible to distinguish between the role of a nation as *actor* and its role as *target*. (See Table 3.)

RELATIONSHIPS BETWEEN INDEPENDENT VARIABLES (POWER, STATUS, BALANCE OF POWER) AND DEPENDENT VARIABLES (COOPERATION/CONFLICT)

Given measures of power, status, balance of power on the one hand and cooperation-conflict on the other, we can now seek to establish relationships between variables. If power, status, and balance of power approaches are valid, one should expect to find the amount of cooperation which a state derives as a function of its (power, status, balance of power) position.

Absolute Theories of Power and Status

The first cluster of theories to be tested links absolute amounts of power or status with the amount of cooperation. According to such hypotheses, if France and England have large stocks of power or status they should either receive a large amount of cooperation or be the recipient of a great deal of hostility from other actors. It is not necessary to report here correlations of 107 power and status variables with cooperation. We shall rather concentrate upon the relationships between the twenty-five variables making up the power index and the amount of cooperation received or given out by each major actor. Interestingly, none of the twenty-five constituents of power showed significant correlations with cooperation for each actor. Table 4 summarizes these results. While France and England evinced the largest percentage of significant correlations between power measures and cooperation measures, not one of the 25 power variables was significantly correlated with cooperation for every

Table 4. Number of Significant Correlations (at .05 or better) between Each of the Twenty-Five Power Variables and the Major Dependent Variables for the Major Powers[a]

Countries	Nation as Actor on Major Power Subsystem (C/C)	Nation as Actor on Entire System (C/C)	Nation as Target of Major Power Subsystem (C/C)	Nation as Target of Entire System (C/C)	Percentage of 25 Variables Significantly Correlated with Dependent Variable
England	0	3	9	4	16%
France	6	6	3	4	19%
Germany	0	0	1	1	2%
Austria-Hungary	1	3	0	0	4%
Russia	0	0	3	3	6%

a. Four major measures of cooperation given and received are presented here and elsewhere. (1) "Nation as actor on major power subsystem" refers to the amount of cooperation a state gives to the four other major powers. (2) "Nation as actor on entire system" refers to the amount of cooperation given by one state to the entire remaining system. (3) "Nation as target of major power system" refers to the amount of cooperation a state receives from the four other major powers. (4) "Nation as target of the entire system" refers to the amount of cooperation a state receives from the rest of the system.

It should be reiterated that cooperation and conflict are the opposite endpoints of a scale. Thus, measures of cooperation are also measures of conflict. High cooperation = low conflict; high conflict = low cooperation. Positive correlations with cooperation are then negative correlations with conflict.

Not one of the 25 power variables was significantly correlated with cooperation/conflict for every nation.

nation. No linkage between absolute amounts of power and cooperation can therefore be established. Further, there is no apparent distinction between power-oriented states and non-power-oriented states. All of the five major states appear to be non-power-oriented and non-power-affected. The results lend no support to absolute theories of power.

What about absolute theories of status? As previously mentioned, there is no truly satisfactory measure of international status. We here employ two surrogate measures: the number of diplomatic recognitions a country receives and the number of foreign diplomats stationed in its territory. The assumption is that high status is indicated by a large number of recognitions and accreditations. The absolute version of status theories would have a nation's position directly affected by its status position. One would anticipate either that a high status nation would receive high cooperation or that it would receive high conflict. The findings, however, as revealed in Table 5 do not bear out any such relationship. Oddly enough the two measures of status often appear to operate inversely: that is, when a nation derives status from recognition, it often does not do so in terms of the number of diplomats stationed within its territory. Germany and Austria-Hungary show opposite signs on the two measures; the Russian pattern is

Table 5. The Relation between Two Status Measures and Cooperation/Conflict

	England	France	Germany	Austria-Hungary	Russia
	n=12	n=12	n=12	n=12	n=12
Status as Measured by Diplomatic Recognition with:					
C/C: Actor on major powers	.35	-.04	-.06	.34	.27
C/C: Actor on system	.12	-.37	-.17	.01	.01
C/C: Target of major powers	.01	.62[a]	-.16	.48	.09
C/C: Target of system	.05	.65[b]	-.15	.38	.02
Status as Measured by Diplomatic Representation with:					
C/C: Actor on major powers	-.09	.62[a]	.31	-.22	.01
C/C: Actor on system	.18	-.42	.40	-.55[a]	-.05
C/C: Target of major powers	.01	.31	.52[a]	-.37	-.27
C/C: Target of system	.23	.35	.52[a]	-.22	-.36

[a] $s \leq .05$

[b] $s \leq .01$

similar to that of Austria; in the case of England and France the record is mixed. Obviously, however, there is no pattern which holds across the diplomatic board, even utilizing a single status measure. Most of the correlations, moreover, are below minimum significance levels. It is perhaps interesting though, that absolute theories of status receive slightly more support than absolute theories of power, even though neither attains significance.

Relative Theories of Power and Status

If absolute theories of power and status cannot be validated during the eighteen seventies, an era typically regarded as the perfection of *Machtpolitik,* are relative formulations of power, status, and balance of power more successful? In this mode, the cooperation (or conflict) received by a state would be the function of its relative position in a ranking of power or status. States with high absolute power, but low power ranking, would in this formulation receive little cooperation (or conflict). To test the power version of relative measures, we employ the 25-variable power index mentioned previously.[4] Since each variable has equal status in the index, the rank for each power consists of a summation of rankings on each variable. (A score of 25 would then be all firsts, a score of 125 all fifths.)[5] The results are depicted in Table 6. Utilizing the power index we can now compare national rankings with cooperation and conflict, that is, we can test a cluster of theories that assert that there is a relationship

Table 6. Rankings on Twenty-Five Variable Power Index, 1870-1881[a]

Year	England Rank/Score	France Rank/Score	Germany Rank/Score	Austria-Hungary Rank/Score	Russia Rank/Score
1870	2 / 67	1 / 60	3 / 75	5 / 93	4 / 84
1871	1(tie)/ 62	1(tie)/ 62	3 / 67	5 / 98	4 / 92
1872	2 / 62	1 / 59	3 / 63	5 /102	4 / 84
1873	1 / 58	2 / 62	3 / 66	5 / 95	4 / 86
1874	1(tie)/ 60	1(tie)/ 60	3 / 65	5 / 94	4 / 91
1875	2 / 65	1 / 58	3 / 68	5 / 94	4 / 89
1876	2 / 63	1 / 58	3 / 66	5 / 96	4 / 88
1877	2 / 64	1 / 62	3 / 68	5 / 85	4 / 83
1878	3 / 70	1 / 60	2 / 62	5 / 95	4 / 81
1879	1(tie)/ 64	1(tie)/ 64	3 / 67	5 / 96	4 / 79
1880	1 / 58	3 / 69	2 / 66	5 / 88	4 / 87
1881	2 / 65	3 / 66	1 / 63	5 / 94	4 / 86

a. France was regarded as the premier military power in Europe before the Franco-Prussian War. After that her primacy waned. She remained superior to both England and Germany in terms of military preparations and expenditure, however, during most of the decade. In economic terms England was ahead of France even at the beginning of the period, and Germany passed her at the end.

between relative power and cooperation in the system. The findings are given in Table 7. These results make clear that power rankings for the five major nations do not account for the amount of cooperation they receive or contribute. Only one significant correlation emerges (for France), and that only in reference to one measure of cooperation. Recurring to Table 6, one notes that French power is trending downward during the decade, that English power is fluctuating and that German power is increasing. But the amount of cooperation that these nations derive bears no relationship to such trends. France receives greater cooperation at the end of the decade (when she is weaker) than she did at the beginning. The German pattern is precisely opposite: she gets more cooperation as she grows in strength. England shows no consistent pattern. The cooperation she receives from others goes steadily downward while her power fluctuates in relation to that of France and Germany. These findings do not appear to corroborate hypotheses concerning the impact of relative power upon cooperation between nations.

Table 7.   Twenty-Five Variable Power Index and Major Dependent
Variables (Cooperation/Conflict Scores)[a]

Variables	Major Power Subsystem	England	France	Germany	Austria-Hungary	Russia
	n=60	n=12	n=12	n=12	n=12	n=12
25-variable power indices with:						
Cooperation/conflict scores: nation as actor on major power subsystem	.01	.44	-.63[b]	.25	--	--
C/C scores: nation as actor on entire system	.09	.26	.24	.16	--	--
C/C scores: nation as target of major power subsystem	-.17	.32	.04	.37	--	--
C/C scores: nation as target of entire system	-.16	.36	-.03	.37	--	--

a. There are no strictly satisfactory correlation measures for this data. The interval cooperation data could have been transformed into ordinal data (with great loss of information) and the two ordinal scales compared by Kendall or Spearman measures. We decided, however, to use a Pearson product-moment measure which probably slightly overstates the degree of association actually present.

No correlations appear for Austria-Hungary and Russia for there is no variation in their ranking during the decade.

b. Significant at .013 level; all other correlations are above the .05 level and insignificant.

If relative power measures do not seem to account for changes in cooperation that nations give or receive individually, it still remains possible that relative balance of power measures, taking alignments into account, may help to explain the amount of total cooperation and conflict in the system. It might be true that when there is a balance of power between alignments, either high cooperation or high conflict is to be expected systemically. Here, therefore, we will be looking not at the amount of cooperation given or received by individual states, but at the average level of cooperation in the system for a particular year. In order to chart such relationships, we shall also have to have a measure of alignments. These have been derived in slightly modified form from Hart (1974). Table 8 offers data on power relationships, alignment patterns and systemic cooperation. The power column shows the amount of power (in terms of rank) of the nations in each grouping (with five as the highest amount of power for any one nation). The cooperation/conflict column gives the amount of systemic cooperation for the year (> 50 = cooperation; < 50 = conflict). The patterns in the table, however, do not show any clear relationship between power balances on the one hand and conflict and cooperation on the other. Neglecting the periods in which cooperative

Table 8.   Balance of Power Patterns and Level of Cooperation/
Conflict in the Major Power Subsystem

Year	International Alignment	Power Alignment	C/C Major Power Subsystem
1870	Germany/France Austria England/Russia	3/10/2	48.406
1871	AFGRE	15	56.805
1872	AFGRE	15	57.118
1873	F/GARE	4/11	57.858
1874	FARE/G	12/3	48.795
1875	FARE/G	12/3	54.334
1876	AFGRE	15	55.186
1877	FAR/E/G	8/4/3	51.654
1878	AGEF/R	13/2	53.814
1879	AGEF/R	13/2	52.464
1880	AFGRE	15	57.381
1881	E/AGR/F	4/8/3	55.394

alignments include all five powers, we have eight years in which counter-balancing coalitions existed. In five of these, 4 v. 1 unbalanced coalitions exist. In each case the power of the single excluded state is dwarfed by that of the remaining four. Yet the amount of systemic cooperation associated with these cases varies enormously. In 1873 the highest amount of general cooperation is recorded in a system characterized by marked power imbalance. Yet in 1874, a year also evincing a great imbalance in power relationships, there is very low systemic cooperation. The other four versus one alignments display moderate cooperation.

There are only two cases where power could be said by any approximation to approach balance. In 1877 and again in 1881 there are 3 v. 1 v. 1 coalitions. These instances are not ones of strict balance as the figures show: the group of three clearly over-balances each of the other two excluded states. Presuming, however, that the excluded two might sometimes work together against the central three, the relationship becomes one of 8 v. 7 units of power. Even these cases, however, do not show a uniform tendency. In 1877 there is a tiny positive net balance of cooperation, verging on indifference. In 1881 cooperation is much higher at the moderate to high end of the spectrum with the same configuration of power. In short, high imbalances of power are associated with both low and high cooperation. There is no definite relationship shown between balance of power and conflict.

If relative power and balance of power measures do not account for patterns of cooperation and conflict in the international system, do status rankings help to do so? It might be hypothesized that the distribution of prestige and reputation is a sensitive predictor of international rivalry. Perhaps states with low prestige will compete with those with high prestige for a more equal share of the benefits. We shall employ two surrogate measures of status: diplomatic accreditations (representation) and diplomatic recognitions. The assumption is that the nation with the highest foreign diplomatic representation and the highest number of diplomatic recognitions will have the greatest prestige and status. Table 9 displays the status rankings on the two measures. As the table shows, however, there is some disjunction between the separate measures. Germany's rise to pre-eminence is most clearly captured in the representation measure, as is France's decline. The possible invalidity of the recognition measure of status is shown most clearly in the Austrian case where Vienna moves from fourth to second in a period of just four years. Again utilizing the recognitions measure, we observe that France appears to gain much greater status during the decade. But the representation measure is also not fully satisfactory. It probably understates Austria's position. The reason may be Vienna's modest economic and commercial potential which translated itself into diminished consular representation.

Table 9. Ranking of Nations on the Two Status Indicators, by Year

Year	England		France		Germany		Austria-Hungary		Russia	
	Status on		Status on		Status on		Status on		Status on	
	Rep.	Rec.	Rep.	Rec.	Rep.	Rec.	Rep.	Rec.	Rep.	Rec.
1870	3	2	1	3	4	1	5	4	2	5
1871	1	2	2	2	4	1	5	4	3	5
1872	2	2	1	3	2	1	5	4	4	5
1873	2	2	1	3	4	1	5	4	3	5
1874	3	1	2	1	1	3	5	3	4	5
1875	3	1	2	1	1	4	5	3	4	5
1876	3	1	2	1	1	4	5	3	4	5
1877	3	2	2	1	1	4	5	2	3	5
1878	3	2	2	1	1	2	5	2	4	5
1879	3	3	2	1	1	2	5	2	4	5
1880	3	4	2	1	1	3	5	2	4	5
1881	3	3	2	1	1	3	5	2	4	5

Table 10 compares four cooperation indicators with the two status measures. Unfortunately, there appears to be no pattern of significant relationships between status rankings and cooperation. Some powers appear to give more cooperation when they have higher status; others give more cooperation when they have less status. There are similar differences in terms of cooperation received. Some powers appear to get more cooperation when they have high status; others receive less cooperation when they have high status. Patterns are slightly more uniform within a single measure, but France is inconsistent on each measure. Certainly no general conclusion can be drawn concerning a specific relationship between status rankings and the amount of cooperation which nations either receive or contribute to others. Again, however, it is interesting to observe that there seems to be a stronger association (be it not uniform) between status measures and cooperation than between power measures and cooperation. This relationship, however, is neither strong enough, nor consistent enough, to be able to claim that relative status measures satisfactorily explain patterns of international cooperation and conflict.

Table 10. Correlations between Rankings on Status and Cooperation/Conflict

	England	France	Germany	Austria-Hungary	Russia
	n=12	n=12	n=12	n=12	n=12
Diplomatic Representation Rankings with:					
C/C: Actor on major powers	.66[b]	-.26	-.18	---	-.07
C/C: Actor on system	.76[b]	.12	-.42	---	.18
C/C: Target of major powers	.52[a]	-.64[b]	-.25	---	-.06
C/C: Target of system	.72[b]	-.69[b]	-.24	---	-.05
Diplomatic Recognition Rankings with:					
C/C: Actor on major powers	-.27	.20	.14	.13	---
C/C: Actor on system	-.16	-.35	.23	-.32	---
C/C: Target of major powers	.13	.67[b]	.39	.02	---
C/C: Target of system	-.07	.72[b]	.38	-.01	---

[a] s ≤ .05

[b] s ≤ .01

Theories Involving Change in Power or Status

Both absolute and relative measures of power and status, however, have a single difficulty: they are static. It is possible rather that nations respond to dynamic factors in the system, to changes in power or status positions. Nations which are increasing in status or power, then, may be expected to stimulate one type of response; nations which are losing power or status to evoke another. If Germany is increasing and France declining, this fact may be much more important than their static positions at any given point in time. Particularly in power terms, historians and political scientists have been wont to claim that the nation which is increasing in power will be the object of most international attention and rivalry (see Doran, 1971). Singer, Bremer and Stuckey (1972) have argued that for the nineteenth century at least, changes toward a further concentration of power were positively correlated with war. Alternatively, it could be argued that a nation increasing its power position might be the beneficiary of an "ingratiation effect" (Healy and Stein, 1973) and derive even more cooperation. Table 11 compares cooperation measures with the change in power position of a nation.

The results, however, do not manifest a central tendency. Changes in power appear to cut in different directions for different countries. Some nations appear to become more involved in conflict because of growing power; others appear to become less involved. The system-wide correlations, moreover, are the least suggestive of significant relationships. There is little evidence supporting theories of change in power as predictors of international conflict and cooperation.

Table 11. Delta of 25-Variable Power Index with Cooperation/Conflict[a]

	System	England	France	Germany	Austria-Hungary	Russia
	n=55	n=11	n=11	n=11	n=11	n=11
Delta of 25-variable power index with:						
C/C: Actor on major powers	.01	.35	-.05	-.01	---	---
C/C: Actor on system	-.02	.14	-.22	.01	---	---
C/C: Target of major powers	.09	.20	-.13	-.33	---	---
C/C: Target of system	.10	.08	.06	-.31	---	---

In the tests of previous clusters of theory, however, it appeared that status measures were slightly more sensitively associated with cooperation than power measures. It therefore might be hoped that dynamic theories of status would offer a satisfactory account of patterns of cooperation and conflict. Table 12 displays correlations between the four cooperation measures and change in status for the five major European powers. There is a prima facie relationship between change in status and German participation in cooperation. Yet, this conclusion is an artifact, because diplomatic representation in Germany and the recognition of Germany were greatly affected by the unification of Germany. Standard sources like the *Almanach de Gotha* do not provide a unified German total until 1874, previously listing Prussia and the other German states separately. Since combining the German states with Prussia results in double-counting (due to internal recognitions), we took Prussian totals from 1870-73, and totals

Table 12. Delta of Two Status Variables with Cooperation/Conflict

	England	France	Germany	Austria-Hungary	Russia
	n=11	n=11	n=11	n=11	n=11
Delta Diplomatic Representation Rank with:					
C/C: Actor on major powers	.24	.03	$-.69^b$	---	.02
C/C: Actor on system	.21	-.24	$-.71^b$	---	-.12
C/C: Target of major powers	.12	.02	$-.62^b$	---	-.12
C/C: Target of system	.16	.02	$-.62^b$	---	-.22
Delta Diplomatic Recognition Rank with:					
C/C: Actor on major powers	-.44	-.14	$.69^b$	.02	---
C/C: Actor on system	-.17	.09	$.65^a$	.05	---
C/C: Target of major powers	-.36	.08	$.64^a$	.23	---
C/C: Target of system	.28	.07	$.67^b$	.05	---

[a] $s \leq .05$

[b] $s \leq .01$

for the unified German Empire from 1874-81. This results in a large decrease in 1874, however, when diplomatic recognitions of Prussia by the smaller German states are no longer counted. In much the same way diplomatic representation in Germany went up when foreign diplomats in the German states were counted as accredited to Germany (also in 1874). Thus, the high correlations which appear are not to be taken as evidence of a real relationship in the data.

Even if the German correlations were taken as significant, however, no relationship between change in status and the amount of cooperation given and received emerges for all countries; sign changes exist for both measures of status. While there appears to be a stronger relationship between change in status and cooperation than change in power and cooperation, it cannot be said that change in status is a satisfactory predictor of the amount of cooperation either in regard to a specific state or to the system as a whole.

Theories Relating the Disparity between Power and Status to the Amount of Cooperation in the System

At this point, the reader may begin to be discouraged: all the clusters of theories tested thus far have failed to demonstrate significant relationships across nations. Neither power nor status in their various forms have accounted for changes in the patterns of cooperation. Could it not be, however, that the failure of previous clusters of theory has been due to their narrowness, and that an approach which considers power and status *in their relationship to each other* might fare better? The theoretical literature would deem it so. Much of the literature of the late sixties and early seventies concentrates upon just such a linkage. In more precise terms, the occurrence of conflict in the system is related to the disparity between power and status, to rank disequilibrium or status inconsistency. Galtung (1964, 1966a, b, c, d) proposes rank disequilibrium as a nearly sufficient condition of aggression. More recently there have been a series of analyses concerned with the systemic consequences of stratification (East, 1969, 1970, 1972; Midlarsky, 1969; Wallace 1970a, 1970b, 1972). The general conclusion of these studies has been that the systemic disparity between power and status is positively correlated with war (East, 1972; Wallace, 1970).

In more traditional terms, such a linkage has frequently been made. Organski's "power transition" theory relates the onset of major war to the attempt of a challenger to catch up with a dominant power. The challenger is stimulated to make his attempt by the disparity between his relatively high power and relatively low status (Organski, 1968a, 1968b). Even

Lenin's theory of imperialism (Lenin, 1917) makes much of the same type of disparity. The reason capitalist alliances can never last and must break down in war is the "uneven development of capitalism." As some states are developing much more rapidly than others, alliances formed at one time on the basis of one power relationship must be forcibly changed as a new economic power relationship emerges. Hence world war. There is therefore a special impetus to testing clusters of theory which relate war or conflict to the discrepancy between power and status. Table 13 presents information on precisely this topic. Twenty-eight status discrepancy variables (disparities between power and status) have been tested against our four measures of cooperation. But again, no pattern holds for all five countries. The significant correlations for one country are not on the same status discrepancy variables as correlations for all other countries. Negative discrepancies between status and power (where power > status) are not more highly correlated with conflict than absolute discrepancies (where power > status *or* status > power). It therefore does not appear that there is a demonstrable relationship between conflict and the disparity between power and status at either the national or the systemic level. [6]

If the reader is inclined to throw up his hands at this point he should by no means do so. Negative findings are as important as positive findings in the development of a discipline, particularly when the propositions questioned are those typically and seriously propounded by other investigators. Eckstein (1974) points out that approximately 30% of articles in physical science journals report negative findings. In this particular case the failure of power and status variables to account for patterns of cooperation and conflict is salient precisely because the conditions for their verification

Table 13. Percentage of Significant Correlations between 28 Status Inconsistency Variables and Cooperation/Conflict

	England	France	Germany	Austria-Hungary	Russia	Total
28 Status Inconsistency Variables (Disparities between Power and Status) and:						
C/C: Actor on major powers	7	0	0	0	0	6%
C/C: Actor on system	7	0	0	0	0	6%
C/C: Target of major powers	0	8	3	1	0	11%
C/C: Target of system	6	9	3	0	0	16%
Totals in %	18%	15%	5%	1%	0%	

were so relatively favorable. The analysis has focussed on a period in history in which historians and political scientists have typically regarded balance of power operations to be at their peak (Hinsley, 1962; Organski, 1968; Doran, 1971). It has centered attention on the major powers, those that might be expected to be most involved in balance of power policies. The data used to confirm or disconfirm power, balance of power and status theories include on the one hand: a wide variety of power measures in economic, industrial, educational, financial, demographic, governmental and military terms; on the other, 2,046 interactions among the great powers reliably scaled in terms of degrees of cooperation and conflict. If power and status propositions were to be supported, it could be assumed prima facie that they would receive their greatest support on the basis of the present study.

The failure of these approaches in the present context leads one to ask how historians, diplomats, and political scientists could so generally have committed themselves to theories which bear such apparently meagre fruit? Is it possible that "power" was misconceived or misinterpreted? That nations which statesmen perceived as "powerful" were not powerful in more objective terms? We have already noted that diplomatic perceptions of power have often been erroneous. Is it possible, indeed, that statesmen attributed high power positions to nations that were aggressive but not particularly powerful? One of the difficulties of pure power and status approaches, of course, is that they neglect the vital question of degree of involvement. A nation may be highly powerful and yet minimally participant in the system; it will evoke much less response (either cooperative or conflictual) than a lesser power which is much more highly involved. While power theories tended to assume that high power meant high participation, the disjunction between them is very marked. This disjunction alone could account for the failure of the four previous clusters of theory.

Theories of the Mode of Exercise of Power

It therefore seems even more relevant to try to find a way of testing the impact of the mode of exercise of power or status upon cooperation and conflict. If attributes like power or status do not explain the amount of cooperation a nation receives, perhaps a variable of more behavioral complexion might remedy the defect. Before such a theoretical variable can be formulated for test, however, it is desirable briefly to review the actual diplomatic employment of power by the major nations in the eighteen seventies. This will give us a clue to the kind of indicator we seek.

We shall look at the diplomatic position and performance of each of the major European powers.

France. During the eighteen seventies, France's diplomacy was in a state of almost total paralysis. She had not yet recovered from the shattering effects of the Franco-Prussian War which led to a pervasive change in her domestic institutions as well as her standing in international diplomacy. According to diplomatic history compilations of significant events, France was the least active of major powers, and she was twice as inactive as her nearest competitor (see Appendix Table A). She also was the target of fewer actions initiated by other states than any other major power (Table B). She made fewer requests or demands than did other states, and rarely received compliance from others. Oddly enough, even though England reverts episodically to "splendid isolation" during the eighteen seventies, Britain was a much more active initiator and responder than France.

This passive status is harder to understand in that France was a very powerful state (see Table 6). Her governmental revenue and expenditures were higher than those of other powers. Her trade surplus was more marked. While in certain categories, like steel and coal production and urban population, she ranked second or third to England and Germany, she spent vast amounts on military preparedness (second only to Russia) and maintained the second largest army in Europe. For most of the decade her position in naval ironclads rivaled Britain's. Her status was also at a peak. In terms of both diplomatic recognition and representation, she was a primary focus of respect and attention (Tables C and D). Yet, given this substantial power and status base, she was very ineffective diplomatically. In terms of cooperation given and received, she ranks last among the five major powers in the European system (Table E). Her position is also ambivalent in regard to other states. She is hostile to some other states, particularly Germany, thus the conflictual amplitude of her policy is high. In sum, France has great power and status, but she is very unsuccessful in capitalizing upon it in practice.

Austria-Hungary. Almost opposite to France is the case of Austria. In terms of both power and status, Austria ranks very low. She is fifth (last) in power; and fourth or fifth in measures of status. Yet her diplomacy is uncommonly effective. She is second only to Germany in the balance of cooperation given and received. She receives more direct cooperation than any other power in the system (Table F). The conflictual amplitude of her policy is low, indicating that she has no fundamental or permanent antagonisms with other states. It is also worth noting that Austria is a member of every majority alignment in the twelve-year period (see Table 8); she is never caught out on a diplomatic or military limb.

Germany. Germany is typically thought to be the center of the European system of the eighteen seventies. This is partly because of her victory over France in 1870-71 and the diplomatic virtuosity of Chancellor Otto von Bismarck. It is certainly true that Germany is a very active power in international relations, ranking first in the number of diplomatic initiatives. She is also very successful in negotiation, achieving the highest return for cooperation given of any state, and ranking second to Austria-Hungary in the amount of direct cooperation received. Her status and power rankings are high and increasing over the decade. If there is any defect in her policy, it is to be found in the estrangement from France occasioned by the seizure of Alsace-Lorraine at the close of the Franco-Prussian War. The continuing hostility toward France ensures that the conflictual amplitude of German policy will be very high: except for France's corresponding score, it is the highest in the European system.

England. England's role in European diplomacy is in part a function of her leadership. Under Gladstone's reform ministry of 1868-74 England played a largely passive, even an aloof role in regard to the continent. During Disraeli's ministry, 1874-1880, however, England took a large part in European affairs, involving herself in the Near Eastern crisis and its settlement at the Congress of Berlin in 1878. British power vied with French and German for paramountcy on the European continent. After Germany took over material leadership in the eighties, England became the major rival. Partly because of the oscillation between isolation and intervention, England was not as successful in European diplomacy as either Austria or Germany, ranking third in the balance of cooperation and fourth in the amount of direct cooperation received.

Russia. Russia was one of the most ineffective powers in the European system. She was highly active, ranking second only to Germany in the number of diplomatic initiatives. In diplomatic effectiveness, however, she was fourth in balance of cooperation, and last in the amount of diplomatic cooperation received. Her case invites comparison with Austria, a state with an even slighter power base. Russia, by virtue of her activity, was often caught in an exposed position with other states ranged against her, as took place in 1877-79. In this same period, she permitted her amplitude to grow, developing conflictual relations with several other states. In comparison to Austria, her policy goes in fits and starts, with amplitude and activity varying greatly from one period to the next (see Table 14). Austria, in contrast, maintains a relatively constant posture of low amplitude and activity for the ten-year period.

Perhaps it is possible to see now why correlational comparisons between power and status, measures, on the one hand, and cooperation, on the other, do not evince any significant relationships. Cooperation can be obtained with low power, provided that is carefully husbanded and exercised. Cooperation can be lost even by powerful states if they do not assert their positions vigorously. Cooperation can also be lost if states permit their conflictual amplitude with others to reach very high levels.[7] In fact, it appears that low power states may gain cooperation if they operate with low amplitude and low activity. Indeed, one of the interesting facets of this study is the degree to which it appears that low power states may sometimes do better than high power states in terms of cooperation gained. Of course, it should be remembered that in the 1870s five major European nations were closely commensurate in power. Even the weaker states, Russia and Austria, could not be taken lightly. Given this rough approximation in power, however, the weaker states often did better than the stronger ones. There may be something in the nature of a premier power position which creates opposition or antagonism.[8] It follows that neither high power nor low power uniformly predicts to cooperation on the international scene. Power measures must be combined with modes of exercise, at least with amplitude and activity, before a reliable theory of cooperation can be derived.

This should give us some guidance to the formulation of a theoretical hypothesis concerning modes of exercise of power. Reviewing the historical cases, one notes that cooperation in the international system can be attained in two different ways:

(1) *High Power, Low Amplitude and High Activity.* The first is through high power, low amplitude and high activity. Germany achieved its best result in terms of cooperation when its activity was high and its conflictual amplitude low. She did less well when either amplitude was higher or activity lower. Even France, a generally unsuccessful state in European diplomacy in this period, received the greatest amount of cooperation when her activity was high and her amplitude low. Britain, on the other hand, did well when her amplitude was high and her activity low. Decreases in amplitude or increases in activity did not lead to any greater degree of cooperation. In this respect, Britain appears as a special case.

(2) *Low Power, Low Amplitude and Low Activity.* A second means to cooperation, however, may be found where power is deficient. Austria is

successful, even outstandingly successful because of her adoption of the maxim: "Don't make waves!" Austria has low policy amplitude and makes certain that she does not fall into a conflictual relationship with any other European state. She even manages to keep on reasonable terms with Russia, her natural rival in the Balkans, by encouraging England to take a leading role in the containment of Russian schemes. Because she has no insistent patterns of antagonism, Austria can afford to be relatively inactive (though not so inactive as France). Given the contrariety of interests in the Balkans, one is astonished to find that Austria receives more direct cooperation from Russia than from any other state in the 1870s. The enormous success of Austrian diplomacy under the Magyar, Count Julius Andrassy, suggests that perhaps some of the Germanocentric accounts of the diplomacy of the period need revision.

In somewhat analogous fashion it appears that cooperation can be lost and conflict engendered in two different ways:

(1) *High Power, High Amplitude and Low Activity*. The first is through high power, high amplitude and low activity. France pursued far too passive a policy after her defeat by Prussia. While Austria-Hungary came back into the European system after her reversal at the hands of Prussia in 1866, France did not. Moreover, she missed many chances to build support for her position. Aside from 1874-5, France did little to seek help against Germany, and offered little in turn to Russia, her logical ally. When Russia needed support at the Congress of Berlin, France did not give it, nor did she give assistance when Russia was casting about for an alternative after the conclusion of the Austro-German Alliance in 1879. We know that a Franco-Russian alliance eventually emerged in 1894, but inactivity in this and other respects was greatly deleterious to French interests from 1871 on. The French also suffered through acceptance of too much conflictual amplitude in their policy. They developed a major antagonism toward Germany, but were not active enough to gain needed cooperation from other powers.

(2) *Low Power, High Amplitude, and High Activity*. A second means to failure and ineffectiveness may be found in a policy of low power, high amplitude and high activity. If high power states can take major initiatory roles in international relations, weaker powers must adhere to more stringent limits. Russia, a relatively weak state, revealed the bankruptcy of her position by an overly active policy in diplomacy. She was second only to Germany in activity, but had far less material power to back up that active policy. She allowed herself to develop patterns of antagonism (particularly with England) that her slender power position could not

sustain. After the Congress of Berlin in 1878 Russia was so vocal and abusive that she drove Bismarck into an anti-Russian alliance with Austria. She received less cooperation than any other major European power for the entire period.

These considerations offer the basis for the formulation of a theory of the exercise of power. This theory should be able to predict when nations will receive and lose cooperation in the international system. It revolves around combinations of three variables: power; conflictual amplitude; and activity. It also rests on three presumptions about the hierarchy of their centrality:

(1) The first presumption is that low power is better than high power, *ceteris paribus* in terms of procuring cooperation.[9]

(2) The second presumption is that low conflictual amplitude is better than high amplitude in terms of procuring cooperation.

(3) The third presumption is that low activity is the appropriate policy for a low power state, but that high activity is appropriate for a high power state.

Eight combinations of the three variables then exist:

Power	Conflictual Amplitude	Activity
Low	Low	Low
Low	Low	High
Low	High	High
Low	High	Low
High	Low	Low
High	Low	High
High	High	High
High	High	Low

These eight combinations can then be ranked according to the explanatory presumptions of the theory in terms of the amount of cooperation they would be expected to produce. This ranking would be as follows:

	Power	Amplitude	Activity	Explanation
1.	Low	Low	Low	Accords with all three presumptions.
2.	High	Low	High	The first presumption

is not meant to require that all low power cases be superior to all high power cases. Low power is superior to high power only where it is at least equivalently exercised. High activity accords with presumption three.

| 3. | Low | Low | High | Amplitude is deemed to |

be more important than activity in producing cooperation.

4.	High	Low	Low
5.	Low	High	Low
6.	High	High	High
7.	Low	High	High
8.	High	High	Low

If this one to eight ranking is correct, the scores of cooperation received should also be distributed in roughly the same order.

Two alternative rankings should also be considered. It is possible that presumption one overstates the case for low power. It might be that low power properly exercised provides the best outcomes in terms of cooperation received, but that high power has certain advantages at the lower end of the scale. High power, therefore, might be a way of avoiding the worst outcomes in terms of cooperation received. If this were true, either cases 7-8 would be reversed or cases 5-6 and 7-8 would be reversed. The alternative rankings then would be:

	II			III	
Low	Low	Low	Low	Low	Low
High	Low	High	High	Low	High
Low	Low	High	Low	Low	High
High	Low	Low	High	Low	Low
Low	High	Low	High	High	High
High	High	High	Low	High	Low
High	High	Low	High	High	Low
Low	High	High	Low	High	High

In order to test this theory of the exercise of power in its three formulations, it is necessary to allocate the data in ways that give a sufficient population of cases under each variable. We have divided the 1870-81 time period into four shorter periods (each with a similar, though not identical population of events):

(1) 1870-73 (where events are sparse);

(2) 1874-76;

(3) 1877-78 (where events are frequent); and

(4) 1879-81.

Table 14 shows these results. Taking the systemic averages in each case as the dividing point between high and low scores, we have Table 15. Given

Table 14. Power, Amplitude and Activity in the
European International System, 1870-1881

	Period	Power[a]	Amplitude[b]	Activity[c]	Cooperation Received[d]
Great Britain	1870-73	62.2	38.1	17	56.7
	1874-76	62.7	40.3	61	52.3
	1877-78	67.0	40.1	113	51.4
	1879-81	62.3	41.7	28	50.8
Germany	1870-73	67.7	33.2	84	53.5
	1874-76	66.3	40.0	65	47.9
	1877-78	65.0	41.8	65	53.0
	1879-81	65.3	42.8	184	55.9
Austria-Hungary	1870-73	97.0	42.3	38	56.8
	1874-76	94.6	41.7	51	56.5
	1877-78	90.0	40.9	58	55.4
	1879-81	92.6	41.6	70	61.4
France	1870-73	60.7	33.4	28	44.1
	1874-76	59.0	40.6	47	53.7
	1877-78	61.0	38.8	14	52.4
	1879-81	66.3	41.4	5	52.3
Russia	1870-73	86.5	41.5	44	56.6
	1874-76	89.3	43.2	104	54.0
	1877-78	82.0	38.6	82	46.5
	1879-81	84.0	41.9	69	50.3

a. Power scores are derived from Table 6, in each case constituting the average for the period in question. High scores denote low power; low scores, high power.

b. Amplitude scores are the average of conflictual actions initiated (the average of all actions below 50, the null or indifference level).

c. Activity scores record the number of actions initiated by the nation in question during the period. This measure is based on historical accounts of significant events.

d. Cooperation received is the average of the scale scores of the events for which the nation is the target. Scores above 50 indicate a net balance of cooperation; scores below 50 indicate a net balance of conflict.

our explanatory theory, it is possible to calculate a relationship between the outcomes predicted by the power exercise hypothesis and the actual outcomes of international diplomacy in the eighteen seventies. Predicted outcomes are ranked on a scale of one to eight. Actual outcomes are given in terms of the cooperation score received. On the basis of the initial version of the hypothesis, a Pearson r of .574 (significance level .004) is achieved. On the basis of version II, a correlation of .615 (significance level .002) is reached. This tends to suggest that the mode of exercise of power may be an even more sensitive predictor of cooperation in the system than the amount of power or status themselves. It also tends to support the notion that behavioral data are more likely to produce relationships with cooperation and conflict, peace and war than attribute data. If this is true, objective power and status theories may have to be reconsidered.

Table 15.   Categorizations of Power, Amplitude
and Activity with Cooperation

	Period	Power	Amplitude	Activity	Cooperation
Great Britain	I	H	H	L	56.7
	II	H	L	L	52.3
	III	H	L	L	51.4
	IV	H	L	L	50.8
Germany	I	H	H	H	53.5
	II	H	H	H	47.9
	III	H	L	H	53.0
	IV	H	L	H	55.9
Austria	I	L	L	L	56.8
	II	L	L	L	56.5
	III	L	L	L	55.4
	IV	L	L	H	61.4
France	I	H	H	L	44.1
	II	H	L	L	53.7
	III	H	H	L	52.4
	IV	H	L	L	52.3
Russia	I	L	L	L	56.6
	II	L	L	H	54.0
	III	L	H	H	46.5
	IV	L	L	H	50.3

Applications of Theory to Practice

It would of course be premature to conclude that gross power is not effective in international affairs and that balances of power are irrelevant to peace or war. Yet it remains surprising that balance of power theories have the hold on informed opinion that they do. At the beginning of the nineteenth and twentieth centuries what was objectionable was not so much that one nation was accumulating a large store of power, but the manner in which that power was being used. Napoleonic France and Wilhelm II's Germany were obnoxious because of the way in which they exercised their power: through wars in the first case and flamboyant crises and demands in the second. Neither power attained the kind of relative predominance which the U.S. enjoyed in 1950; yet, both provoked much more opposition.

To put it shortly, it does not follow that the most powerful nation in the world must automatically engage in the greatest conflict; nor does it follow that lesser states will avoid provoking such conflict. The image of power held by statesmen has unfortunately been an undifferentiated amalgam of both power and practice. Aggressive states have seemed powerful because they were aggressive. Much more powerful states have seemed less powerful because they were quiescent. Merely to take the example of Japan is to see this truth. The Japanese were much less powerful relative to their possible competitors in 1941 than they are today. But today few worry about Japanese power because of the way in which it is exercised. Soviet Russia is much more powerful today than she was in 1945-47 when her intransigence and ostensible aggressiveness brought on the Cold War. European states and the United States are far less worried by her position, because of the relative moderation of her policies. Nazi Germany, on the other hand, was probably less strong in relation to potential opponents than the Kaiser's Germany of 1914. Both Russia and America had emerged on the world scene as stronger international contenders. Yet Germany preoccupied the attention of the world, not because of her overweening power, but because of the use she made of it. Power does not automatically translate itself into aggressiveness.

The eighteenth and nineteenth century applications were similar. Frederick the Great commanded the weakest major state in Europe in both 1740 and 1756; yet this weakness did not stop Prussian expansionism. In 1800 Napoleonic France was stronger relative to opponents, but she undertook wars against leagued powers far stronger than France. Inevitably she was defeated. Yet in 1850, Britain, at the peak of her powers and predominant economically, did not seek to exercise them in a major war with continental states. Nor did the United States in 1910 when she had outstripped all European nations and had an industrial plant more than equal to her two most formidable rivals.

The failure of power analyses leads one to ask why states seek to expand aggressively if power is not the primary motivation? Why should one state challenge another? Organski (1968) argues that states undertake expansion when they are deprived of what they believe to be their fair share of status rewards and when their power enables them to make such a challenge. The strongest states do not have to be aggressive, they already have won the rewards of prestige and status. Very weak states cannot risk a challenge. The up-and-coming powers which are yet inferior in strength and deficient in prestige are the logical candidates for aggression. Yet it is no more true that rapidly developing second-rank states are expansionist than it is that first-rank nations utilize their power in aggression. The United States passed Britain, Germany and Russia in power without making a frontal military challenge. In the nineteenth century Britain passed France without military conflict.

In short there probably is no answer in strict power or status terms to the question of aggression. Often it seems that powers which foresee a radical decline in their own position if they do not strike are the ones most tempted to launch an attack. And this attack may take place almost regardless of the force ranged against them. Predicted decline may then be a greater stimulus to expansion than anticipated growth in power.[10]

Today, powers can no longer afford the luxury of military aggression against major opponents. Whether military success has been the vehicle for greater cooperation in the past (and it probably has not), it is certainly a mixed blessing in the present. If the lessons of theories of the exercise of power are to be taken seriously, one might hazard the opinion that one crucial variable for strong states is conflictual amplitude. Regardless of their power, such states are not likely to win positive rewards of cooperation from other members of the system unless they simultaneously reduce the conflict they express to most external rivals. Both the United states and the Soviet Union improved their positions internationally when they reduced the conflictual tone and application of their policies.

If amplitude is important, so is activity. One of the errors of American diplomacy in the nineteen twenties and thirties was to assume that if the United States became inactive in world affairs, its interests would contract accordingly so that its net position would improve. But if strong friendships and animosities are entertained, inactivity cannot serve national interest. Only active participation will suffice. Indeed, if interests are to be protected and cooperation gained, amplitude must be reduced far more than activity.

None of these strictures should be read as suggesting that power is unimportant in international affairs. If national policy requires a long and difficult agenda of action, power is the necessary, though it may not be the sufficient, condition of success. If the agenda is shorter, great power may not even be a necessary condition. As we have seen, Austria-Hungary achieved a great deal with little power relative to her competitors. The same conditions probably hold with greater force today.

In future, the world will probably witness an interaction of four or five major units: United States, Russia, Japan, W. Europe, and China. This interaction will be much more fluid than the bipolarity of recent vintage. It is therefore likely that conflictual policy amplitude will be reduced in comparison with its cold war equivalent. Alignments will take place with a shifting series of candidates: such fluidity will be inhibited if specific antagonisms retain their prior strength. The rules of the game will have some similarity to those of the eighteen seventies. If so, diplomacy and alignment will have a much greater role than they have had in the recent past. The central position, the role of "honest broker," will be sought by a number of nations. Its assignment may even go to nations or units whose power would not appear to justify such a status. As in the eighteen seventies, however, the mode of exercise of power is likely to be more important than power itself.

NOTES

1. On absolute bases, states with large stocks of power would all receive large amounts of cooperation (or conflict); on relative bases a nation ranked fourth in the power or status hierarchy would get very little cooperation even thought it might have very large absolute stocks.

2. The reverse may also be true: when historical sources were compared with newspaper accounts of European international relations in 1875 it was found that the extremes of the "war-scare" crisis occurring in that year were missed in newspaper accounts because the crisis was one of cabinet diplomacy (Gray, 1971).

3. In many cases, the category variables were highly intercorrelated. For example, only four of ten educational measures were necessary to capture the variety of the educational variables.

4. We do not claim that such an index would offer intuitively satisfying results for each period of modern diplomatic or contemporary history, but we do claim that it validly represents power relationships for the 1870s.

5. This procedure, of course, assumes a simple ratio scale of 1 through 5 in our rankings. Although this scale will not correspond to the actual degrees of difference among the nations on the power variables, it does correspond to the hierarchy of precedence that statesmen themselves perceive and employ in their dealings with one another. In other words, national leaders think in terms of first, second, third and so on, not in terms of degrees of differences among nations on each power dimension. The power index, moreover, makes possible the comparison of status and power rankings for each state. Our findings utilizing the 25-variable index, moreover, are quite conclusive. It is unlikely that a more refined ratio scale, differentiating differences on each variable, would give alternative results.

6. It should be noted that Ray (1974) found a similar result when he sought to determine whether the nations suffering the greatest status discrepancy were also those most involved in conflict: they were not.

7. This, of course, is not a logical consequence of high conflictual amplitude. According to one version of the deterrent hypothesis, conflict on the part of one state (the deterror) will be returned by cooperation on the part of another (the deterree).

8. This conclusion receives support from British historian A. J. P. Taylor (1954).

9. This presumption would accord with typical balance of power approaches.

10. This formulation covers the Austrian and German motivations in World War I and the Japanese motivations in World War II.

REFERENCES

ABELL, P. (1970) "Some problems in the theory of structural balance: towards a theory of structural strain," pp. 389-411 in M. Lane (ed.) Introduction to Structuralism. New York: Basic Books.

––– (1968) "Structural balance in dynamic structures." Sociology 2, 3: 333-352.

ABRAMSON, E., H. A. CUTLER, R. W. KAUTZ, and M. MENDLESON (1958) "Social power and commitment: a theoretical statement." American Sociological Rev. 23, 1: 15-22.

ADAMS, J. S. (1965) "Inequity in social exchange," in L. Berkowitz (ed.) Advances in Experimental Social Psychology, Volume 2. New York: Academic Press.

ADAMS, J. S. and A. K. ROMNEY (1959) "A functional analysis of authority." Psychology Rev. 66, 4: 234-251.

ALBERTINI, L. (1952) The Origins of the War of 1914. London: Oxford Univ. Press.

ALBRECHT-CARRIÉ, R. (1970) Britain and France: Adaptations to a Changing Context of Power. Garden City, New York: Doubleday.

ALCOCK, N. Z. (1970) "An empirical measure of internation threat: some preliminary implications for the Middle East conflict." Peace Research Society (International) Papers 15: 51-72.

ALCOCK, N. Z. and A. G. NEWCOMBE (1970) "The perception of national power." Journal of Conflict Resolution 14, 3: 335-343.

ALGER, C. and S. J. BRAMS (1967) "Patterns of representation in national capitals and intergovernmental organizations." World Politics 19, 4: 646-663.

ALGOSAIBI, G. A. R. (1965) "The theory of international relations: Hans J. Morgenthau and his critics." Background 8: 221-256.

ALKER, H. R., JR. and P. G. BOCK (1972) "Propositions about international relations: contributions from the International Encyclopedia of the Social Sciences," pp. 385-496 in J. A. Robinson (ed.) Political Science Annual, Volume III. New York: Bobbs-Merrill.

ALKER, H. R., JR. and B. RUSSETT (1964) "On measuring inequality." Behavioral Science 9, 3: 207-218.

ALTMAN, I. and J. E. MC GRATH (1966) Small Group Research: A Synthesis and Critique of the Field. New York: Holt, Rinehart and Winston.

American Historical Association (1961) Guide to Historical Literature. New York: Macmillan.

ARON, R. (1966) Peace and War: A Theory of International Relations. Garden City, New York: Doubleday.

ASH, M. A. (1951) "An analysis of power with special reference to international politics." World Politics 3, 2: 218-237.

AZAR, E. E. and J. D. BEN-DAK (1974 forthcoming) [eds.] Theory and Practice of Events Research: Studies in Internation Actions and Interactions. New York: Gordon and Breach.

AZAR, E. E., R. A. BRODY, and C. A. McCLELLAND (1972) "International events interaction analysis: some research considerations." Sage Professional Paper in International Studies 1, 1. Beverly Hills and London: Sage Publications.

AZAR, E. (1970) "Analysis of international events." Peace Research Reviews 4, 1.

BACHRACH, P. and M. S. BARATZ (1962) "Two faces of power." American Political Science Rev. 56, 4: 947-952.

BALDWIN, D. A. (1971a) "The costs of power." Journal of Conflict Resolution 15, 2: 145-155.

--- (1971b) "Inter-nation influence revisited." Journal of Conflict Resolution 15, 4: 471-486.

--- (1971c) "The power of positive sanctions." World Politics 24, 1: 19-38.

--- (1971d) "Thinking about threats." Journal of Conflict Resolution 15, 1: 71-78.

BANKS, A. S. (1971) Cross-Polity Time Series Data. Cambridge, Massachusetts: The MIT Press.

BANKS, A. S. and P. M. GREGG (1965) "Grouping political systems: q-factor analysis of a cross-polity survey." American Behavioral Scientist 9, 3: 3-6.

BANTON, M. (1965) [ed.] Political Systems and the Distribution of Power. London: Tavistock.

BARBER, B. (1957) Social Stratification: A Comparative Analysis of Structure and Process. New York: Harcourt, Brace and World.

BARNETT, A. D. (1970) "The new multipolar balance in East Asia: implication for United States policy," Annales 390 (July) 73-86.

BEER, F. A. (1970) Alliances: Latent War Communities in the Contemporary World. New York: Holt, Rinehart and Winston.

BELL, C. (1971) The Conventions of Crisis: A Study in Diplomatic Management. London: Oxford Univ. Press.

--- (1962) Negotiation from Strength: A Study in the Politics of Power. London: Chatto and Windus.

BELL, R., D. V. EDWARDS, and R. H. WAGNER (1969) Political Power: A Reader in Theory and Research. New York: The Free Press.

BENDIX, R. (1952) "Social stratification and political power." American Political Science Rev. 46, 2: 357-375.

BENDIX, R. and S. M. LIPSET (1966) [eds.] Class, Status and Power, second edition. New York: The Free Press.

BENNIS, W. G., N. BERKOWITZ, M. AFFINITO, and M. MALONE (1958) "Authority, power, and the ability to influence." Human Relations 11, 2: 143-155.

BENOIT-SMULLYAN, E. (1944) "Status, status types and status interrelations. American Sociological Rev. 9 (April): 151-161.

BERELSON, B. and G. A. STEINER (1964) Human Behavior: An Inventory of Scientific Findings. New York: Harcourt, Brace and World.

BERNSTEIN, R. A. and P. D. WELDON (1968) "A structural approach to the analysis of international relations." Journal of Conflict Resolution 12 (June): 159-181.

BIERSTADT, R. (1950) "An analysis of social power." American Sociological Rev. 15 (December): 730-738.

BLAKE, R. R. and J. S. MOUTON (1961) "The experimental investigation of interpersonal influence," pp. 216-276 in A. D. Biderman and H. Zimmer (eds.) The Manipulation of Human Behavior. New York: Wiley.

BLAU, P. M. (1964) Exchange and Power in Social Life. New York: Wiley.

BOULDING, K. (1963) "Toward a pure theory of threat systems." American Economic Rev. 53, 2: 424-434.

--- (1962) Conflict and Defense: A General Theory. New York: Harper.

BRAMS, S. J. (1969a) "The search for structural order in the international system: some models and preliminary results." International Studies Quarterly 13, 3: 254-280.

――― (1969b) "The structure of influence relationships in the international system," pp. 583-599 in J. N. Rosenau (ed.) International Politics and Foreign Policy, second edition. New York: The Free Press.

――― (1968) "Measuring the concentration of power in political systems." American Political Science Rev. 62, 2: 461-475.

――― (1966) "Transaction flows in the international system." American Political Science Rev. 60, 4: 880-898.

BROOM, L. and L. F. JONES (1970) "Status consistency and political preference: the Australian case." American Sociological Rev. 35, 6: 989-1101.

BRUCAN, S. (1971) The Dissolution of Power: A Sociology of International Relations. New York: Knopf.

BRZEZINSKI, Z. (1972) "The balance of power delusion." Foreign Policy, 7 (Summer): 54-59.

BULL, H. (1971) "The new balance of power in Asia and the Pacific." Foreign Affairs 49, 4: 669-681.

BURGESS, P. M. and R. W. LAWTON (1972) "Indicators of international behavior: an assessment of events data research." Sage Professional Paper in International Studies 1, 10. Beverly Hills and London: Sage Publications.

BURGESS, P. M. and D. W. MOORE (1972) "Inter-nation alliances: an inventory and appraisal of propositions," pp. 339-384 in J. A. Robinson (ed.) Political Science Annual, Volume III. New York: Bobbs-Merrill.

BURNS, A. L. (1972) "Scientific and strategic-political theories of international politics," pp. 56-85 in B. Porter (ed.) The Aberystwyth Papers: International Politics, 1919-1969. London: Oxford Univ. Press.

――― (1957) "From balance of power to deterrence: a theoretical analysis." World Politics 9, 4: 494-529.

BURR, R. N. (1965) "By reason or force: Chile and the balancing of power in South America, 1830-1905." University of California, Berkeley, Publications in History, Volume 77, October 9.

――― (1955) "The balance of power in nineteenth-century South America: an exploratory essay." The Hispanic American Historical Rev. 35 (February): 37-60.

BURTON, J. W. (1966) "Conflict as a function of change," pp. 370-401 in A. de Reuck and J. Knight (eds.) Conflict in Society. London: J. and A. Churchill.

BUTTERFIELD, H. (1966) "The balance of power," pp. 132-148 in H. Butterfield and M. Wight (eds.) Diplomatic Investigations. London: George Allen and Unwin.

BUTTERFIELD, H. and M. WIGHT (1966) [eds.] Diplomatic Investigations: Essays in the Theory of International Politics. London: George Allen and Unwin.

CARLTON, W. G. (1947) "Ideology or balance of power." Yale Rev. 36, 4: 590-602.

CARR, E. H. (1939) The Twenty Years' Crisis, 1919-1939: An Introduction to the Study of International Relations. London: Macmillan.

CARROLL, B. A. (1972) "Peace research: the cult of power." Journal of Conflict Resolution 16, 4: 585-616.

CARTWRIGHT, D. (1965) "Influence, leadership, control," pp. 1-47 in J. G. March (ed.) Handbook of Organizations. Chicago: Rand McNally.

――― (1959a) "A field theoretical conception of power," pp. 183-220 in D. Cartwright (ed.) Studies in Social Power. Ann Arbor: Univ. of Michigan Press, Institute for Social Research.

――― (1959b) "Power: a neglected variable in social psychology," pp. 1-14 in D. Cartwright (ed.) Studies in Social Power. Ann Arbor: Univ. of Michigan Press, Institute for Social Research.

CARTWRIGHT, D. and F. HARARY (1956) "Structural balance: a generalization of Heider's theory." Psychology Rev. 63, 5: 277-293.

CHAMPLIN, J. R. (1971) [ed.] Power. New York: Atherton Press.

——— (1970) "On the study of power." Politics and Society 1, 1: 91-111.

CHATTERJEE, P. (1972) "The classical balance of power theory." Journal of Peace Research 1: 51-61.

CHERTOK, E. (1955) "Sources of international tension." Bulletin of the Research Exchange on the Prevention of War 3, 17.

CHOUCRI, N. and R. C. NORTH (1974 forthcoming) Nations in Conflict: Population, Expansion and War. San Francisco: W. H. Freeman.

——— (1972) "Alternative dynamics of international conflict: population, resources, technology and some implications for policy." World Politics 24 (Spring): 80-122.

——— (1969) "The determinants of international violence." Peace Research Society (International) Papers 12: 33-63.

CLARK, K. B. (1965) "Problems of social power and social change: a relevant social psychology." Journal of Social Issues 21, 3: 4-20.

CLARK, T. N. (1967) "The concept of power: some overemphasized and under-emphasized dimensions." Southwest Social Science Quarterly 48, 3: 271-286.

CLAUDE, I. L., JR. (1962) Power and International Relations. New York: Random House.

——— (1961) "The management of power in the changing United Nations." International Organization 15, 2: 219-235.

COBB, R. W. and C. ELDER (1970) International Community: A Regional and Global Study. New York: Holt, Rinehart and Winston.

CORSON, W. H. (1970) "Measuring conflict and cooperation intensity in east-west relations: a manual and codebook." Ann Arbor: Univ. of Michigan, Institute for Social Research.

COSER, L. (1956) The Functions of Social Conflict. Glencoe, Illinois: Free Press.

COX, R. W. and H. K. JACOBSON (1973) [eds.] The Anatomy of Influence: Decision Making in International Organization. New Haven: Yale Univ. Press.

CRESPIGNY, A. DE (1968) "Power and its forms." Political Studies 16 (June): 192-205.

DAHL, R. A. (1968) "Power," pp. 405-415 in International Encyclopedia of the Social Sciences, Volume XII. New York: Free Press.

——— (1957) "The concept of power." Behavioral Science 2, 3: 201-215.

DAHL, R. A. and C. E. LINDBLOM (1953) Politics, Economics, and Welfare. New York: Harper and Row.

DAHLSTROM, E. (1966) "Exchange, influence, and power." Acta Sociologica 9, 3-4: 237-284.

DAVIS, J. A. (1967) "Clustering and structural balance in graphs." Human Relations 20, 2: 181-187.

DAVIS, K. (1954) The Demographic Foundations of National Power. New York: Van Nostrand.

DAVISON, W. P. (1959) Power—The Idea and its Communication. Santa Monica, California: The RAND Corporation, P-1869.

DEHIO, L. (1962) The Precarious Balance: Four Centuries of the European Power Struggle, translated from the German by C. Fullman. New York: Random House.

DENTON, F. H. (1969) Factors in International System Violence. Santa Monica, California: The RAND Corporation, P-4216.

DEUTSCH, K. W. (1968) The Analysis of International Relations. Englewood Cliffs, New Jersey: Prentice-Hall.

――― (1967) "On the concepts of politics and power," pp. 48-57 in J. C. Farrell and A. P. Smith (eds.) Theory and Reality in International Relations. New York: Columbia Univ. Press.

――― (1966a) "On theories, taxonomies, and models as communication codes for organizing information." Behavioral Science 11 (January): 1-17.

――― (1966b) "Power and communication in international society," pp. 300-316 in A. De Reuck and J. Knight (eds.) Conflict in Society. London: J. and A. Churchill.

――― (1963) The Nerves of Government. New York: Free Press.

――― (1960) "Toward an inventory of basic trends and patterns in comparative and international politics." American Political Science Rev. 54, 1: 34-57.

DEUTSCH, K. W. and J. D. SINGER (1964) "Multipolar power systems and international stability." World Politics 16, 3: 390-406.

DORAN, C. F. (1973) "Hierarchic regionalism from the core state perspective: the U.S. case," in W. D. Chittick (ed.) The Analysis of Foreign Policy Outcomes. New York: Merrill.

――― (1971) The Politics of Assimilation: Hegemony and its Aftermath. Baltimore: The Johns Hopkins Press.

DOREIAN, P. (1969) "Interaction under conditions of crisis: applications of graph theory to international relations." Peace Research Society (International) Papers 9: 89-107.

DOWTY, A. (1971) "Foreign-linked factionalism as a historical pattern." Journal of Conflict Resolution 15, 4: 429-442.

DROR, Y. (1971) Crazy States: A Counterconventional Strategic Problem. Lexington, Massachusetts: Heath Lexington Books.

EAST, M. A. (1972) "Status discrepancy and violence in the international system: an empirical analysis," pp. 299-319 in J. N. Rosenau, V. Davis and M. East (eds.) The Analysis of International Politics. New York: Free Press.

――― (1970) "Rank-dependent interaction and mobility: two aspects of international stratification." Peace Research Society (International) Papers 14: 113-127.

――― (1969) Stratification and International Politics. Ph.D. dissertation. Princeton: Princeton Univ. Press.

EAST, M. A. and P. M. GREGG (1967) "Factors influencing cooperation and conflict in the international system." International Studies Quarterly 11 (September): 244-269.

EASTON, D. (1956) "Limits of the equilibrium model in social research." Behavioral Science 1, 2: 96-104.

――― (1953) The Political System. New York: Alfred Knopf.

ECKSTEIN, H. (1974 forthcoming) "The critical case study" in Frederick Greenstein and Nelson Polsby (eds.) Handbook of Political Science. Reading, Massachusetts: Addison-Wesley.

ELDER, R. E. (1950) "Factors affecting stability of the balance of power." Western Political Quarterly 3, 2: 155-160.

EMERSON, R. M. (1964) "Power-dependence relations: two experiments." Sociometry 27, 3: 282-298.

――― (1962) "Power-dependence relations." American Sociological Rev. 27 (February): 31-40.

EMMET, D. (1953-1954) "The concept of power." Proceedings of the Aristotelian Society 54: 1-26.

ETZIONI, A. (1961) A Comparative Analysis of Complex Organizations. New York: Free Press.

FALEY, T. and J. T. TEDESCHI (1971) "Status and reactions to threats." Journal of Personality and Social Psychology 17, 2: 192-199.

FAY, S. B. (1938) The Origins of the World War. New York: Macmillan.

––– (1930) "Balance of power," pp. 395-399 in International Encyclopedia of the Social Sciences, Volume II. New York: Macmillan.

FEELEY, M. (1970) "Coercion and compliance: a new look at an old problem." Law and Society Review 4: 505-519.

FLAMENT, C. (1963) Applications of Graph Theory to Group Structure. Englewood Cliffs, New Jersey: Prentice-Hall.

FLIESS, P. J. (1966) Thucydides and the Politics of Bipolarity. Baton Rouge: Louisiana State Univ. Press.

FORSYTHE, M. G., H. M. A. KEENS-SOPER, and P. SAVIGEAR (1970) [eds.] The Theory of International Relations: Selected Texts from Gentili to Treitschke. New York: Atherton Press.

FOSSUM, E. (1967) "Factors influencing the occurrence of military coups d'etat in Latin America." Journal of Peace Research 3: 225-251.

FRENCH, J. R. P. (1956) "A formal theory of social power." Psychology Rev. 63, 3: 181-194.

FRENCH, J. R. P., H. W. MORRISON, and G. LEVINGER (1960) "Coercive power and forces affecting conformity." Journal of Abnormal and Social Psychology 61, 1: 93-101.

FRENCH, J. R. P., and B. RAVEN (1959) "The bases of social power," pp. 159-167 in D. Cartwright [ed.] Studies in Social Power. Ann Arbor: Univ. of Michigan, Institute for Social Research.

FRIEDMAN, J. R., C. BLADEN, and S. ROSEN (1970) [eds.] Alliance in International Politics. Boston: Allyn and Bacon.

FUCKS, W. (1965) Formeln zur Macht. Stuttgart: Deutsch Verlagsawfalt.

GALTUNG, J. (1966a) "East-West interaction patterns." Journal of Peace Research 2: 146-177.

––– (1966b) "International relations and internation conflicts: a sociological approach." Transaction of the Sixth World Congress of Sociology 1 (September): 121-161.

––– (1966c) "Rank and social integration: a multidimensional approach," pp. 145-198 in J. Berger, M. Zelditch, and B. Anderson (eds.) Sociological Theories in Progress. Boston: Houghton-Mifflin.

––– (1966d) "Small group theory and the theory of international relations: a study in isomorphism," pp. 270-302 in M. A. Kaplan (ed.) New Approaches to International Relations. New York: St. Martin's Press.

––– (1965) "Institutionalized conflict resolution." Journal of Peace Research 4: 348-397.

––– (1964a) "Balance of power and the problem of perception: a logical analysis." Inquiry 7, 3: 277-294.

––– (1964b) "A structural theory of aggression." Journal of Peace Research 2: 95-119.

––– (1964c) "Summit meetings and international relations." Journal of Peace Research 1: 36-54.

GAREAU, F. H. (1962) [ed.] The Balance of Power and Nuclear Deterrence. Boston: Houghton Mifflin.

GARTHOFF, R. L. (1951) "The concept of the balance of power in Soviet policy making." World Politics 4, 1: 85-111.

GEORGE, A. L., D. K. HALL, and W. R. SIMONS (1971) The Limits of Coercive Diplomacy: Laos, Cuba, Vietnam. Boston: Little, Brown.

GERMAN, F. C. (1960) "A tentative evaluation of world power." Journal of Conflict Resolution 4, 1: 138-144.

GIDDENS, A. (1968) " 'Power' in the recent writing of Talcott Parsons." Sociology 2, 3: 257-272.

GILPIN, R. (1972) "Has modern technology changed international politics?" pp. 166-174 in J. N. Rosenau, V. Davis, and M. East (eds.) The Analysis of International Politics. New York: Free Press.

GLEDITSCH, N. P. (1970) "Rank theory, field theory, attribute theory: three approaches to interaction in the international system." Dimensionality of Nations Project Research Report 47, Univ. of Hawaii.

――― (1969) "Rank and interaction: a general theory with some application to the international system." Presented at the Third Conference of the International Peace Research Association, Karlovy Vary, Czechoslovakia, September 21-23.

――― (1967) "Trends in world airline patterns." Journal of Peace Research 4: 366-408.

GLENN, N. D., J. P. ALSTON, and D. WEINER (1970) Social Stratification: A Research Bibliography. Berkeley: The Glendessary Press.

GLOCK, C. Y. (1956) "Issues that divide: a postscript." Journal of Social Issues 12, 3: 40-43.

GOFFMAN, I. W. (1957) "Status consistency and preference for change in power distribution." American Sociological Rev. 22, 3: 275-281.

GOLDHAMER, H. and E. SHILS (1939) "Types of power and status." American Journal of Sociology 45, 2: 171-182.

GOODMAN, R., J. HART, and R. ROSECRANCE (1974 forthcoming) "Testing inter-nation theory: methods and data in a situational analysis of international politics," in E. E. Azar and J. D. Ben-Dak (eds.) Theory and Practice of Events Research: Studies in Internation Actions and Interactions. New York: Gordon and Breach.

GOULDNER, A. W. (1960) "The norm of reciprocity: a preliminary statement." American Sociological Rev. 25, 2: 161-178.

GRAY, B. (1971) "The London Times vs. diplomatic history: a comparison of two event sources." Unpublished mimeo. Cornell Univ.

GREGG, P. M. and A. S. BANKS (1965) "Dimensions of political systems: factor analysis of a cross polity survey." American Political Science Rev. 59, 3: 602-614.

GROSS, F. (1963) "Tension areas analysis." Il Politico 28 (March): 45-60.

GUETZKOW, H. (1957) "Isolation and collaboration: a partial theory of internation relations." Journal of Conflict Resolution 1 (March): 48-68.

GULICK, E. V. (1960) "Our balance of power system in perspective." Journal of International Affairs 14, 1: 9-20.

――― (1955) Europe's Classical Balance of Power: A Case History of the Theory and Practice of One of the Great Concepts of European Statecraft. Ithaca, New York: Cornell Univ. Press.

――― (1943) The Balance of Power. Philadelphia: Pacifist Research Bureau.

HAAS, E. B. (1953a) "The balance of power as a guide to policy-making." Journal of Politics 15, 3: 370-398.

——— (1953b) "The balance of power: prescription, concept or propaganda?" World Politics 5, 4: 442-477.

HAAS, M. (1970) "International subsystems: stability and polarity." American Political Science Rev. 63, 1: 98-123.

——— (1965a) "A functional approach to international organization." Journal of Politics 27, 3: 498-517.

——— (1965b) "Societal approaches to the study of war." Journal of Peace Research 4: 307-323.

HAINES, R. L. (1971a) "The balance-of-power system in Europe," pp. 9-32 in L. Graymer (ed.) Systems and Actors in International Politics. San Francisco: Chandler.

——— (1971b) "A century of system change," pp. 33-66 in L. Graymer (ed.) Systems and Actors in International Politics. San Francisco: Chandler.

HANRIEDER, W. F. (1966) "International organizations and international systems." Journal of Conflict Resolution 10, 3: 297-313.

——— (1965) "The international system: bipolar or multibloc." Journal of Conflict Resolution 9 (September): 299-308.

HARARY, F. (1961) "A structural analysis of the situation in the Middle East in 1956." Journal of Conflict Resolution 5 (June): 167-178.

——— (1953-1954) "On the notion of balance of a signed graph." Michigan Mathematical Journal 2: 143-146.

HARARY, F. and H. MILLER (1970) "A graph-theoretic approach to the analysis of international relations." Journal of Conflict Resolution 14 (March): 57-63.

HARARY, F., R. Z. NORMAN, and D. CARTWRIGHT (1965) Structural Models: An Introduction to the Theory of Directed Graphs. New York: Wiley.

HARRIS, E. E. (1957) "Political power." Ethics 68, 1: 1-10.

HARSANYI, J. C. (1962a) "Measurement of social power in n-person reciprocal power situations." Behavioral Science 7, 1: 81-91.

——— (1962b) "Measurement of social power, opportunity costs, and the theory of two-person bargaining games." Behavioral Science 7, 1: 67-80.

HART, J. (1974 forthcoming) "Symmetry and polarization in the European international system, 1870-1879." Journal of Peace Research 1.

HARTMANN, F. H. (1973) The Relations of Nations, fourth edition. New York: Macmillan.

HAVENER, T. and A. PETERSON (1974 forthcoming) "Measuring conflict and cooperation in international relations: a methodological inquiry," in E. E. Azar and J. D. Ben-Dak (eds.) Theory and Practice of Events Research: Studies in Internation Actions and Interactions. New York: Gordon and Breach.

HEALY, B. (1973) Economic Power Transition in the International System: The Translation of Economic Power into Political Leverage in the International Monetary System. Ph.D. dissertation. Ithaca, New York: Cornell Univ.

HEALY, B. and A. STEIN (1973) "The balance of power in international history: theory and reality." Journal of Conflict Resolution 17, 1: 33-62.

HEIDER, F. (1958) The Psychology of Interpersonal Relations. New York: Wiley.

——— (1946) "Attitudes and cognitive organizations." Journal of Psychology, 21 (January): 107-112.

HERMANN, C. F. (1972) [ed.] International Crises: Insights from Behavioral Research. New York: Free Press.

HERZ, J. H. (1960) "Balance systems and balance policies in a nuclear and bipolar age." Journal of International Affairs 19, 1: 35-48.

HEWITT, J. P. (1970) Social Stratification and Deviant Behavior. New York: Random House.

HINSLEY, F. H. (1971) "The development of the European states system since the eighteenth century," pp. 284-294 in G. H. Quester (ed.) Power, Action and Interaction: Readings on International Politics. Boston: Little, Brown.

––– (1963) Power and the Pursuit of Peace: Theory and Practice in the History of Relations between States. Cambridge: Cambridge Univ. Press.

HIRSCHMAN, A. O. (1945) National Power and the Structure of Foreign Trade. Berkeley and Los Angeles: Univ. of California Press.

HOFFMANN, S. (1972a) "Weighing the balance of power." Foreign Affairs 50, 4: 618-643.

––– (1972b) "Will the balance balance at home?" Foreign Policy 7 (Summer): 60-86.

––– (1968) "Balance of power," pp. 506-510 in International Encyclopedia of the Social Sciences, Volume I. New York: Free Press.

––– (1963) "Discord in community: the North Atlantic area as a partial international system." International Organization 17, 3: 521-549.

––– (1960) [ed.] Contemporary Theory in International Relations. Englewood Cliffs, New Jersey: Prentice-Hall.

––– (1959) "International relations: the long road to theory." World Politics 11, 3: 346-377.

HOLBRAAD, C. (1970) The Concert of Europe: A Study in German and British International Theory. London: London Group.

HOLSTI, K. J. (1972) International Politics: A Framework for Analysis, second edition. Englewood Cliffs, New Jersey: Prentice-Hall.

––– (1970) "National role conceptions in the study of foreign policy." International Studies Quarterly 14, 3: 233-309.

––– (1964) "The concept of power in the study of international relations." Background 7, 4: 179-194.

––– (1963) "The use of objective criteria for the measurement of international tension levels." Background 7 (August): 77-95.

HOLSTI, O. R. (1972) Crisis Escalation War. Montreal: McGill-Queen's Univ. Press.

––– (1963) "The value of international tension measurement." Journal of Conflict Resolution 7, 3: 608-617.

HOMANS, G. C. (1958) "Social behavior as exchange." American Journal of Sociology 63, 6: 597-606.

HOWARD, M. (1964) "Military power and international order." International Affairs 40 (July): 397-408.

HULL, C. (1948) Memoirs. New York: Macmillan.

HUNTER, R. E. (1972-1973) "Power and peace." Foreign Policy 9 (Winter): 37-54.

HURWITZ, J. I., A. F. ZANDER, and B. HYMOVITCH (1968) "Some effects of power on the relations among group members," pp. 291-297 in D. Cartwright and A. Zander (eds.) Group Dynamics: Research and Theory, third edition. New York: Harper.

INSKO, C. A. (1967) Theories of Attitude Change. New York: Appleton-Century-Crofts.

JACKSON, E. (1966) "Status consistency and symptoms of stress," pp. 21-28 in R. Bendix and S. M. Lipset (eds.) Class, Status and Power: Social Stratification in Comparative Perspective. New York: Free Press.

JAMES, A. (1964) "Power politics." Political Studies 12, 3: 307-326.

JENSEN, L. (1965) "Military capabilities and bargaining behavior." Journal of Conflict Resolution 9, 2: 155-163.

JONES, S. B. (1954) "The power inventory and national strategy." World Politics 6, 4: 421-452.

JOUVENEL, B. DE (1949) On Power. New York: Viking.

KADT, E. J. DE (1965) "Conflict and power in society." International Social Science Journal 17, 3: 454-471.

KADUSHIN, C. (1968) "Power, influence and social circles: a new methodology for studying opinion makers." American Sociological Rev. 33 (October): 685-698.

KAPLAN, A. (1964) "Power in perspective," pp. 11-32 in R. Kahn and E. Boulding (eds.) Power and Conflict in Organizations. New York: Basic Books.

KAPLAN, M. A. (1968) [ed.] New Approaches to International Relations. New York: St. Martin's Press.

--- (1966) "Some problems of international systems research," pp. 469-501 in International Political Communities—An Anthology. Garden City, New York: Doubleday.

--- (1960) "Theoretical inquiry and the balance of power," pp. 19-39 in Yearbook of World Affairs 1960. London: Stevens.

--- (1957a) "Balance of power, bipolarity and other models of international systems." American Political Science Rev. 51, 3: 684-695.

--- (1957b) System and Process in International Politics. New York: Wiley.

KAPLAN, M. A., A. L. BURNS, and R. E. QUANDT (1960) "Theoretical analysis of the balance of power." Behavioral Science 5, 3: 240-252.

KARLSSON, G. (1962) "Some aspects of power in small groups," in J. H. Criswell, H. Solomon, and P. Suppes (eds.) Mathematical Methods in Small Group Processes. Stanford: Stanford Univ. Press.

KIMBERLEY, J. C. (1966) "A theory of status equilibration," in J. Berger, M. Zelditch, and B. Anderson (eds.) Sociological Theories in Progress, Volume I. Boston: Houghton Mifflin.

KINDLEBERGER, C. P. (1970) Power and Money. New York: Basic Books.

--- (1959) "International political theory from outside," pp. 69-82 in W. T. R. Fox (ed.) Theoretical Aspects of International Relations. Notre Dame, Indiana: Univ. of Notre Dame Press.

KISSINGER, H. (1957) A World Restored: Metternich, Castlereagh, and the Problems of Peace. Boston: Houghton Mifflin.

KLEIN, D. H. (1959) Germany's Economic Preparations for War. Cambridge: Harvard Univ. Press.

KLING, M. (1962) "Towards a theory of power and political instability in Latin America," pp. 123-139 in J. H. Kautsky (ed.) Political Change in Underdeveloped Countries. New York: Wiley.

KLINGBERG, F. L. (1941) "Studies in measurement of the relations among sovereign states." Psychometrika 6, 6: 335-352.

KNORR, K. (1972) "Notes on the analysis of national capabilities," pp. 175-186 in J. N. Rosenau, V. Davis, and M. East (eds.) The Analysis of International Politics. New York: Free Press.

--- (1970) Military Power and Potential. Lexington, Massachusetts: D. C. Heath

--- (1968) "Military power potential," pp. 325-332 in International Encyclopedia of the Social Sciences, Volume X. New York: Free Press.

––– (1966) On the Uses of Military Power in the Nuclear Age. Princeton: Princeton Univ. Press.

––– (1957) "The concept of economic potential for war." World Politics 10, 1: 49-62.

––– (1956) The War Potential of Nations. Princeton: Princeton Univ. Press.

KOVACS, A. F. (1957) "The balance of power." Thought Patterns 5: 1-19.

KUHN, A. (1964) "Bargaining power in transactions: a basic model of interpersonal relationships." American Journal of Economics and Sociology 23 (January): 49-63.

LAGOS, G. (1963) International Stratification and Underdeveloped Countries. Chapel Hill, North Carolina: Univ. of North Carolina Press.

LANGER, W. (1969) Explorations in Crisis: Papers on International History, edited by C. E. and E. Schorske. Cambridge: Belknap Press of Harvard Univ. Press.

––– (1951) The Diplomacy of Imperialism 1890-1902, second edition. New York: Knopf.

––– (1950) European Alliances and Alignments 1871-1890, second edition. New York: Random House.

LASSWELL, H. D. and A. KAPLAN (1950) Power and Society: A Framework for Political Inquiry. New Haven: Yale Univ. Press.

LEHMANN, E. W. (1969) "Toward a macro-sociology of power." American Sociological Rev. 34 (August): 453-465.

LENIN, V. I. (1917) Imperialism: The Highest Stage of Capitalism. Boston: Progress Printing Company.

LENSKI, G. (1954) "Status crystallization: a non-vertical dimension of social status." American Sociological Rev. 19, 4: 405-413.

LEPAWSKY, A., E. H. BUEHRIG, and H. D. LASSWELL (1971) The Search for World Order: Studies by Students and Colleagues of Quincy Wright. New York: Appleton-Century-Crofts.

LEVI, W. (1969) "War and the quest for national power," pp. 35-38 in D. G. Pruitt and R. C. Snyder (eds.) Theory and Research on the Causes of War. Englewood Cliffs, New Jersey: Prentice-Hall.

LEWIN, K. (1951) Field Theory in Social Science. New York: Harper.

LIPPITT, R., N. POLANSKY, and S. ROSEN (1952) "The dynamics of power." Human Relations 5, 1: 37-64.

LISKA, G. (1963) "Continuity and change in international systems." World Politics 16, 1: 118-136.

––– (1962) Nations in Alliance: The Limits of Interdependence. Baltimore: Johns Hopkins Press.

––– (1957) International Equilibrium: A Theoretical Essay on the Politics and Organization of Security. Cambridge: Harvard Univ. Press.

McCLELLAND, C. A. (1966) Theory and the International System. New York: Macmillan.

McINTOSH, D. S. (1963) "Power and social control." American Political Science Rev. 57, 3: 619-631.

MacIVER, R. M. (1964) Power Transformed. New York: Macmillan.

MACK, R. W. and R. C. SNYDER (1957) "The analysis of social conflict–toward an overview and synthesis." Journal of Conflict Resolution 1, 2: 212-248.

MANSERGH, N. (1949) The Coming of the First World War: A Study in the European Balance, 1878-1914. London: Longmans, Green.

MARCH, J. G. (1966) "The power of power," pp. 39-70 in D. Easton (ed.) Varieties of Political Theory. Englewood Cliffs, New Jersey: Prentice-Hall.

——— (1957) "Measurement concepts in the theory of influence." Journal of Politics 19, 2: 202-226.

——— (1956) "Influence measurement in experimental and semiexperimental groups." Sociometry 19, 4: 260-271.

——— (1955) "An introduction to the theory and measurement of influence." American Political Science Rev. 49, 2: 431-451.

MASTERS, R. D. (1961) "A multi-bloc model of the international system." American Political Science Rev. 55, 4: 780-798.

MAURSETH, P. (1964) "Balance-of-power thinking from the Renaissance to the French Revolution." Journal of Peace Research 1: 120-136.

MAZUR, A. (1968) "A nonrational approach to theories of conflict and coalitions." Journal of Conflict Resolution 12, 2: 196-205.

MERRIAM, C. E. (1964) Political Power: Its Composition and Incidence. New York: Collier.

MIDLARSKY, M. (1969) Status Inconsistency and the Onset of International Warfare. Ph.D. dissertation. Evanston, Illinois: Northwestern Univ.

MILLER, R. C. (1964) "Some comments on power on the international level." Background 7, 4: 195-200.

MINOGUE, K. R. (1959) "Power in politics." Political Studies 7, 3: 269-289.

MODELSKI, G. (1964a) "Decentralization of authority and concentration of power in international systems." Princeton Univ. Center of International Studies (mimeo).

——— (1964b) "Kautilya: foreign policy and international system in the ancient Hindu world." American Political Science Rev. 68, 3: 549-560.

——— (1961) "International relations and area studies: the case of South East Asia." International Relations 2 (April): 143-155.

MOORE, W. E. (1966) "Global sociology: the world as a singular system." American Journal of Sociology 71 (March): 475-482.

MORGENTHAU, H. J. (1973) Politics Among Nations: The Struggle for Power and Peace, fifth edition. New York: Alfred A. Knopf.

——— (1958) "Power as a political concept," pp. 66-77 in R. Young (ed.) Approaches to the Study of Politics. Evanston, Illinois: Northwestern Univ.

——— (1946) Scientific Man vs. Power Politics. Chicago: Univ. of Chicago Press.

MORISSETTE, J. O. (1958) "An experimental study of the theory of structural balance." Human Relations 11, 3: 239-254.

MOSES, L. E., R. A. BRODY, O. R. HOLSTI, J. B. KADANE, and J. S. MILSTEIN (1967) "Scaling data on inter-nation action." Science 156 (May 26): 1054-1059.

MUELLER, J. E. (1968) Deterrence, Numbers and History. Los Angeles: Univ. of California, Security Studies Paper 12.

MULDER, M. (1960) "The power variable in communication experiments." Human Relations 13, 3: 241-257.

MULDER, M., R. VAN DIJK, T. STELWAGEN, J. VERHAGEN, S. SOUTENDIJK, and J. ZWEZERIJNEN (1966) "Illegitimacy of power and positivity of attitudes toward the power person." Human Relations 19 (February): 21-37.

NAGEL, J. H. (1968) "Some questions about the concept of power." Behavioral Science 13, 2: 129-137.

NEUMANN, F. L. (1950) "Approaches to the study of political power." Political Science Quarterly 65, 2: 161-180.

NEWMAN, W. J. (1968) The Balance of Power in the Interwar Years, 1919-1939. New York: Random House.

NICHOLSON, M. B. and P. A. REYNOLDS (1967) "General systems, the international system, and the Eastonian analysis." Political Studies 15 (February): 12-31.

NORTH, R. C. and N. CHOUCRI (1968) "Background conditions to the outbreak of the First World War." Peace Research Society (International) Papers 9: 125-137.

NYE, J. S., JR. (1968) "Comparative regional integration: concept and measurement." International Organization 22 (Autumn): 855-880.

OGLEY, R. (1971) "Investigating the effects of threats." Peace Research Society (International) Papers 16: 61-93.

ORGANSKI, A. F. K. (1968a) "Power transition," pp. 415-418 in International Encyclopedia of the Social Sciences, Volume XII. New York: Free Press.

––– (1968b) World Politics, second edition. New York: Knopf.

OSGOOD, R. (1961) "The use of military power," pp. 1-21 in R. A. Goldwin (ed.) America Armed. Chicago: Rand McNally.

PARENTI, M. (1970) "Power and pluralism: a view from the bottom." Journal of Politics 32, 3: 501-530.

PARK, T. (1972) "The role of distance in international relations: a new look at the social field theory." Behavioral Science 17, 4: 337-348.

PARSONS, T. (1964) "Some reflections on the place of force in social process," pp. 33-70 in H. Eckstein (ed.) Internal War. New York: Free Press.

––– (1963a) "On the concept of influence." Public Opinion Quarterly 27, 1: 37-62, 87-92.

––– (1963b) "On the concept of political power." Proceedings of the American Philosophical Society 107 (June): 232-262.

PARTRIDGE, P. H. (1963) "Some notes on the concept of power." Political Studies 11, 2: 107-125.

PATEL, J. J. (1964) "The economic distance between nations: its origin, measurement and outlook." The Economic Journal 74 (March): 119-131.

PATTERSON, J. (1969) "Corporate behavior and balance of power: some uses of the structural approach." Business Horizons 12 (June): 39-60.

PEARSON, F. (1970) "Interaction in an international political subsystem: the Middle East, 1963-1964." Peace Research Society (International) Papers 15: 73-99.

PEN, J. (1971) "Bilateral monopoly, bargaining and the concept of economic power," pp. 97-115 in K. W. Rothschild (ed.) Power in Economics. Baltimore: Penguin.

PENROSE, E. F. (1965) The Revolution in International Relations: A Study in the Changing Nature and Balance of Power. London: F. Cass.

––– (1964) "Political development and the intra-regional balance of power." Journal of Development Studies 1, 1: 47-70.

PETERSEN, I. D. (1968) "An ecological model for the analysis of power." Cooperation and Conflict 3, 2: 131-147.

PETERSSON, H. F. (1964) Power and International Order: An Analytical Study of Four Schools of Thought and their Approaches to the War, the Peace and a Post-War System 1914-1919. Lund: Skanska Centraltryckeriet.

PHILLIPS, W. R. (1971) "The dynamics of behavioral action and reaction in international conflict." Peace Research Society (International) Papers 17: 31-46.

PLATT, J. (1970) "Hierarchical restructuring." General Systems 15: 49-54.

POLLARD, A. F. (1923) "The balance of power." Journal of the British Institute of International Affairs 2 (March): 51-64.

POOL, I. DE S. (1965) "Deterrence as an influence process," pp. 189-196 in D. G. Pruitt and R. C. Snyder (eds.) Theory and Research on the Causes of War. Englewood Cliffs, New Jersey: Prentice-Hall.

PRUITT, D. G. (1966) "Reward structure and its effect on cooperation." Peace Research Society (International) Papers 5: 73-85.

——— (1964) "National power and international responsiveness." Background 7, 4: 165-178.

——— (1962) "An analysis of responsiveness between nations." Journal of Conflict Resolution 6 (March): 5-18.

QUESTER, G. H. (1966) Deterrence before Hiroshima: The Airpower Background of Modern Strategy. New York: Wiley.

RANSOM, H. H. (1968) "International relations." Journal of Politics 30, 2: 345-371.

RAVEN, B. H. and J. R. P. FRENCH, JR. (1958) "Legitimate power, coercive power, and observability in social influence." Sociometry 21, 2: 83-97.

RAVEN, B. H. and A. W. KRUGLANSKI (1970) "Conflict and power," pp. 69-109 in P. G. Swingle (ed.) The Structure of Conflict. New York: Academic Press.

RAY, J. L. (1974) Status Inconsistency and War Involvement among European States, 1816-1970. Ph.D. dissertation. Ann Arbor: Univ. of Michigan.

REINKEN, D. L. (1968) "Computer explorations of the 'balance of power': a project report," pp. 459-482 in M. A. Kaplan (ed.) New Approaches to International Relations. New York: St. Martin's Press.

REINTON, P. O. (1967) "International structure and international integration: the case of Latin America." Journal of Peace Research 4: 334-365.

REUCK, A. DE and J. KNIGHT (1966) [eds.] Conflict in Society. London: J. and A. Churchill.

REYNOLDS, P. A. (1971) An Introduction to International Relations. Longman: Longman Group.

RIGGS, F. W. (1961) "International relations as a prismatic system," pp. 144-181 in K. Knorr and S. Verba (eds.) The International System: Theoretical Essays. Princeton: Princeton Univ. Press.

RIKER, W. H. (1964) "Some ambiguities in the notion of power." American Political Science Rev. 58, 2: 341-349.

——— (1962) The Theory of Political Coalitions. New Haven: Yale Univ. Press.

RILEY, J. A. (1969) "An application of graph theory to social psychology." Lecture notes in Mathematics: The Many Facets of Graph Theory #110. New York and Berlin: Springer-Verlag.

ROBINSON, J. A. (1969) "Crisis decision-making: an inventory and appraisal of concepts, theories, hypotheses, and techniques of analysis," pp. 111-148 in J. A. Robinson (ed.) Political Science Annual, Volume II. New York: Bobbs-Merrill.

ROBINSON, T. W. (1969) "Systems theory and the communist system." International Studies Quarterly 13, 4: 398-420.

ROSECRANCE, R. (1973) International Relations: Peace or War? New York: McGraw-Hill.

——— (1966) "Bipolarity, multipolarity, and the future." Journal of Conflict Resolution 10, 3: 314-327.

——— (1963) Action and Reaction in World Politics: International Systems in Perspective. Boston: Little, Brown.

——— (1961) "Categories, concepts, reasoning in international relations." Behavioral Science 6, 3: 222-231.

ROSECRANCE, R. and J. E. MUELLER (1967) "Decision-making and the quantitative analysis of international relations," pp. 1-19 in Yearbook of World Affairs 1967. London: Stevens and Sons.

ROSEN, S. (1957) "An approach to the study of aggression." Journal of Social Psychology 46 (November): 259-267.

ROSEN, S. (1970) "A model of war and alliance," pp. 215-237 in J. R. Friedman, C. Bladen, and S. Rosen (eds.) Alliance in International Politics. Boston: Allyn and Bacon.

ROSENAU, J. N., V. DAVIS, and M. A. EAST (1972) [eds.] The Analysis of International Politics: Essays in Honor of Harold and Margaret Sprout. New York: Free Press.

ROTHSTEIN, R. (1968) Alliances and Small Powers. New York: Columbia Univ. Press.

——— (1966) "Alignment, nonalignment and small powers: 1945-1965." International Organization 20 (Summer): 397-418.

RUMMEL, R. J. (1972a) Dimensions of Nations. Beverly Hills, California: Sage Publications, Inc.

——— (1972b) "U.S. foreign relations: conflict, cooperation and attribute distances," pp. 71-114 in B. M. Russett (ed.) Peace, War, and Numbers. Beverly Hills, California: Sage Publications, Inc.

——— (1971) "A status-field theory of international relations." Dimensionality of Nations Project Research Report 50, Univ. of Hawaii.

——— (1969a) "Field and attribute theories of nation behavior: some mathematical interrelationships." Dimensionality of Nations Project Research Report 31, Univ. of Hawaii.

——— (1969b) "Indicators of gross national and international patterns." American Political Science Rev. 63, 1: 127-147.

——— (1967) "A synthesis of formal and functional regions using a general field theory of spatial behavior," in B. J. L. Berry and D. F. Marbel (eds.) Spatial Analysis. Englewood Cliffs, New Jersey: Prentice-Hall.

——— (1966a) "The dimensionality of nations project," in R. L. Merritt and S. Rokkan (eds.) Comparing Nations. New Haven: Yale Univ. Press.

——— (1966b) "A social field theory of foreign conflict behavior." Peace Research Society (International) Papers 4: 131-150.

——— (1966c) "Some dimensions in the foreign behavior of nations." Journal of Peace Research 3: 201-224.

——— (1964) "Testing some possible predictors of conflict behavior within and between nations." Peace Research Society (International) Papers 1: 76-111.

RUSSELL, B. (1938) Power: A New Social Analysis. New York: Norton.

RUSSETT, B. M. (1968a) "Components of an operational theory of international alliance formation." Journal of Conflict Resolution 12, 3: 285-301.

——— (1968b) "Delineating international regions," pp. 317-352 in J. D. Singer (ed.) Quantitative International Politics: Insights and Evidence. New York: Free Press.

——— (1967) International Regions and the International System: A Study in Political Ecology. Chicago: Rand McNally.

——— (1963) "Toward a model of competitive international politics." Journal of Politics 25 (May): 226-247.

––– (1962) "Cause, surprise, and no escape." Journal of Politics 24 (February): 3-22.

RUSSETT, B. M., H. R. ALKER, JR., K. W. DEUTSCH, and H. D. LASSWELL (1964) World Handbook of Political and Social Indicators. New Haven: Yale Univ. Press.

RUSSETT, B. M. and W. C. LAMB (1968) "Global patterns of diplomatic exchange, 1963-1964." Journal of Peace Research 1: 37-55.

SAID, A. A. (1968) [ed.] Theory of International Relations: The Crisis of Relevance. Englewood Cliffs, New Jersey: Prentice-Hall.

SAMPSON, E. E. (1969) "Studies of status congruence," pp. 225-270 in L. Berkowitz (ed.) Advances in Experimental Social Psychology, Volume IV. New York: Academic Press.

SAWYER, J. (1967) "Dimensions of nations: size, wealth, and politics." American Journal of Sociology 73 (September): 145-172.

SCHELLING, T. C. (1966) Arms and Influence. New Haven: Yale Univ. Press.

––– (1960) The Strategy of Conflict. Cambridge: Harvard Univ. Press.

SCHERMERHORN, R. A. (1961) Society and Power. New York: Random House.

SCHOPLER, J. (1965) "Social power," pp. 177-219 in L. Berkowitz (ed.) Advances in Experimental Social Psychology, Volume II. New York: Academic Press.

SCHWARTZMAN, S. (1965) "International development and international feudalism: the Latin American case," pp. 52-77 in Proceedings of the International Peace Research Association Conference, Groningen, Netherlands, July 3-5.

SCHWARTZMAN, S. and M. M. Y. ARAUJO (1966) "The images of international stratification in Latin America." Journal of Peace Research 3: 225-243.

SCHWARZENBERGER, G. (1967) "From bipolarity to multipolarity?" pp. 179-185 in Yearbook of World Affairs 1967. London: Stevens and Sons.

––– (1965) "Beyond power politics?" pp. 223-234 in Yearbook of World Affairs 1965. London: Stevens and Sons.

––– (1964) Power Politics: A Study of International Society, third edition. New York: Praeger.

SCOTT, A. (1967) The Functioning of the International System. New York: Macmillan.

––– (1956) "Challenge and response: a tool for the analysis of international affairs." Review of Politics 18, 2: 207-226.

SEABURY, P. (1965) [ed.] Balance of Power. San Francisco: Chandler.

SHIMBORI, M., H. IKEDA, T. ISHIDA, and M. KONDO (1963) "Measuring a nation's prestige." American Journal of Sociology 69 (July): 63-68.

SIGLER, J. H., J. O. FIELD, and M. L. ADELMAN (1972) "Applications of events data analysis: cases, issues, and programs in international interaction." Sage Professional Paper in International Studies 1, 2.

SIMON, H. A. (1953) "Notes on the observation and measurement of political power." Journal of Politics 15, 4: 500-516.

SINGER, J. D. (1972) "The 'correlates of war' project: interim report and rationale." World Politics 24, 2: 243-270.

––– (1969) "The global systems and its subsystems: a developmental view," in J. N. Rosenau (ed.) Linkage Politics: Essays on the Convergence of National and International Systems. New York: Free Press.

––– (1965) [ed.] Human Behavior and International Politics: Contributions from the Social-Psychological Sciences. Chicago: Rand McNally.

——— (1963) "Inter-nation influence: a formal model." American Political Science Rev. 57, 2: 420-430.

SINGER, J. D., S. BREMER, and J. STUCKEY (1972) "Capability, distribution, uncertainty, and major power war, 1820-1965," pp. 19-48 in B. Russett (ed.) Peace, War and Numbers. Beverly Hills, California: Sage Publications, Inc.

SINGER, J. D. and M. SMALL (1968) "Alliance aggregation and the onset of war, 1815-1945," pp. 247-286 in J. D. Singer (ed.) Quantitative International Politics. New York: Free Press.

——— (1966a) "The composition and status ordering of the international system: 1815-1940." World Politics 18, 2: 236-283.

——— (1966b) "National alliance commitments and war involvement, 1815-1945." Peace Research Society (International) Papers 5: 109-140.

SMALL, M. and J. D. SINGER (1973) "The diplomatic importance of states, 1816-1970." World Politics 25, 4: 577-599.

SMITH, C. G. (1971) [ed.] Conflict Resolution: Contributions of the Behavioral Sciences. Notre Dame: Univ. of Notre Dame Press.

SNYDER, G. H. (1965) "The balance of power and the balance of terror," pp. 184-201 in P. Seabury (ed.) Balance of Power. San Francisco: Chandler.

——— (1961) Deterrence and Defense: Toward a Theory of National Security. Princeton: Princeton Univ. Press.

——— (1960a) "Balance of power in the missile age." Journal of International Affairs 14, 1: 21-34.

——— (1960b) "Deterrence and power." Journal of Conflict Resolution 4, 2: 163-178.

SNYDER, R. C. (1955) "Toward greater order in the study of international politics." World Politics 7, 3: 461-478.

SPIEGEL, S. L. (1970) "Bimodality and international order: the paradox of parity." Public Policy 18, 3: 383-412.

SPYKMAN, N. J. (1942) "U.S. foreign policy and the balance of power." The Review of Politics 1 (January): 76-83.

SULLIVAN, D. G. (1963) Towards an Inventory of Basic Propositions in Contemporary Textbooks in International Relations. Ph.D. dissertation. Evanston, Illinois: Northwestern Univ.

TANNENBAUM, A. S. (1962) "An event structure approach to social power and to the problem of power comparability." Behavioral Science 7, 3: 315-331.

TANNENBAUM, F. (1952) "The balance of power versus the coordinate state." Political Science Quarterly 67, 2: 173-197.

——— (1946) "The balance of power in society." Political Science Quarterly 61, 4: 481-504.

TANTER, R. (1966) "Dimensions of conflict behavior within and between nations, 1958-1960." Journal of Conflict Resolution 10 (March): 41-64.

TAYLOR, A. J. P. (1954) The Struggle for Mastery in Europe 1848-1918. New York: Oxford Univ. Press.

TAYLOR, C. L. and M. C. HUDSON (1972) World Handbook of Political and Social Indicators, second edition. New Haven: Yale Univ. Press.

TAYLOR, H. F. (1970) Balance in Small Groups. New York: Van Nostrand Reinhold.

TEDESCHI, J. T. (1972) The Social Influence Processes. Chicago: Aldine-Atherton.

——— (1970) "Threats and promises," pp. 155-191 in P. Swingle (ed.) The Structure of Conflict. New York: Academic Press.

TEDESCHI, J. T., T. V. BONOMA, and R. C. BROWN (1971) "A paradigm for the study of coercive power." Journal of Conflict Resolution 15, 2: 197-223.

TEDESCHI, J. T., T. V. BONOMA, B. R. SCHLENKER, and S. LINDSKOLD (1970) "Power, influence, and behavioral compliance." Law and Society Rev. 4, 4: 521-545.

TEDESCHI, J. T., B. R. SCHLENKER, and T. V. BONOMA (1973) Conflict, Power and Games. Chicago: Aldine-Atherton.

TEDESCHI, J. T., B. R. SCHLENKER, and S. LINDSKOLD (1972) "The exercise of power and influence," in J. T. Tedeschi (ed.) The Social Influence Processes. Chicago: Aldine-Atherton.

THOMPSON, K. W. (1960) Political Realism and the Crisis of World Politics. Princeton: Princeton Univ. Press.

——— (1959) "American approaches to international politics," pp. 205-235 in Yearbook of World Affairs 1959, Volume XIII. London: Stevens and Sons.

——— (1958) "The limits of principle in international politics: necessity and the new balance of power." Journal of Politics 20, 3: 437-467.

THOMPSON, W. R. (1973) "The regional subsystem: a conceptual explication and a propositional inventory." International Studies Quarterly 17, 1: 89-117.

——— (1970) "The Arab sub-system and the feudal pattern of interaction: 1965." Journal of Peace Research 2: 151-167.

TUCKER, R. W. (1958) "Force and foreign policy." Yale Rev. 47, 3: 374-392.

——— (1952) "Professor Morgenthau's theory of political 'realism.'" American Political Science Review 46, 1: 214-224.

TUMIN, M. M. (1967) Social Stratification: The Forms and Functions of Inequality. Englewood Cliffs, New Jersey: Prentice-Hall.

VAGTS, A. (1948) "The balance of power: growth of an idea." World Politics 1, 1: 82-101.

VAN DOORN, J. A. A. (1962-1963) "Sociology and the problem of power." Sociologia Neerlandica 1, 1: 3-51.

VAYRYNEN, R. (1971) "On the definition and measurement of small power status." Cooperation and Conflict 6, 2: 91-102.

——— (1970) "Stratification in the system of international organization." Journal of Peace Research 4: 291-309.

VINCENT, J. E. (1972a) "An application of attribute theory to General Assembly voting patterns and some implications." International Organization 26, 3: 551-582.

——— (1972b) "Comments on social field theory." Dimensionality of Nations Project Research Report 58, Univ. of Hawaii.

——— (1971a) Factor Analysis in International Relations: Interpretation, Problem Areas and an Application. Gainesville: Univ. of Florida Press.

——— (1971b) "Predicting voting patterns in the General Assembly." American Political Science Rev. 65, 2: 421-498.

——— (1971c) "Scaling the universe of states on certain useful multivariate dimensions." Journal of Social Psychology 85 (December): 261-283.

——— (1970) "An analysis of caucusing group activity at the United Nations." Journal of Peace Research 2: 133-150.

——— (1968a) "National attributes as predictors of delegate attitudes at the United Nations." American Political Science Rev. 62, 3: 916-931.

——— (1968b) "Systematic analysis of national attributes." Comparative Political Studies 1, 3: 431-435.

VINCENT, J. E. with J. L. FALARDEAU, E. W. SCHWERIN, B. L. BOZEMAN, and R. E. JEDNAK (1971) "Generating some empirically based indices for international alliance and regional systems operating in the early 1960s." International Studies Quarterly 15, 4: 465-525.

VITAL, D. (1967) The Inequality of States: A Study of the Small Power in International Relations. Oxford: Clarendon Press.

VON DEN BERGHE, P. L. (1960) "Distance mechanisms of stratification." Sociology and Social Research 44, 3: 155-164.

VON GENTZ, F. (1906) Fragments on the Balance of Power. London: Peltier.

WALLACE, M. (1973) War and Rank among Nations. Lexington, Massachusetts: Lexington Books.

--- (1972) "Status, formal organization, and arms levels as factors leading to the onset of war, 1820-1964," pp. 49-70 in B. M. Russett (ed.) Peace, War, and Numbers. Beverly Hills, California: Sage Publications, Inc.

--- (1971) "Power, status, and international war." Journal of Peace Research 1: 22-35.

--- (1970) "Status inconsistency, vertical mobility, and international war, 1825-1964." Ph.D. dissertation. Ann Arbor: Univ. of Michigan.

WALTER, B. (1964) "On the logical analysis of power-attribution procedures." Journal of Politics 26, 4: 850-866.

WALTER, E. V. (1964) "Power and violence." American Political Science Rev. 58, 2: 350-360.

--- (1959) "Power, civilization, and the psychology of conscience." American Political Science Rev. 53, 3: 641-661.

WALTZ, K. N. (1967) "International structure, national force, and the balance of world power," pp. 31-47 in J. C. Farrell and A. P. Smith (eds.) Theory and Reality in International Relations. New York: Columbia Univ. Press.

--- (1965) "Contention and management in international relations." World Politics 17, 4: 720-744.

--- (1964) "The stability of a bipolar world." Daedalus 93 (Summer): 881-909.

WASSERMAN, B. (1959) "The scientific pretensions of Professor Morgenthau's theory of power politics." Australian Outlook 13, 1: 55-70.

WESOLOWSKI, W. (1966) "Some notes on the functional theory of stratification," pp. 64-68 in R. Bendix and S. M. Lipset (eds.) Class, Status and Power, second edition. New York: Free Press.

WIGHT, M. (1973) "The balance of power and international order: Essays in Honour of C. A. W. Manning. London: Oxford Univ. Press.

--- (1966) "The balance of power," pp. 149-175 in H. Butterfield and M. Wight (eds.) Diplomatic Investigations. London: Allen and Unwin.

--- (1946) Power Politics. London: Royal Institute of International Affairs.

WOLFERS, A (1959) "The balance of power." SAIS Review 3, 3: 9-16.

--- (1951) "The pole of power and the pole of indifference." World Politics 4, 1: 39-63.

WOODHEAD, A. G. (1970) Thucydides on the Nature of Power. Martin Classical Lectures, Volume XXIV. Cambridge: Harvard Univ. Press.

WRIGHT, Q. (1966) "Approaches to the understanding of international politics," pp. 61-83 in E. H. Buehrig (ed.) Essays in Political Science. Bloomington: Indiana Univ. Press.

--- (1955) The Study of International Relations. New York: Appleton-Century-Crofts.

––– (1942) A Study of War, two volumes. Chicago: The Univ. of Chicago Press.

YOUNG, O. R. (1969) The Politics of Force: Bargaining during International Crisis. Princeton: Princeton Univ. Press.

––– (1968a) "Political discontinuities in the international system." World Politics 20, 3: 369-392.

––– (1968b) A Systemic Approach to International Politics. Princeton University Center of International Studies Research Monograph 33.

ZARTMAN, I. W. (1967) "Africa as a subordinate state system in international relations." International Organization 21, 3: 545-564.

ZELDITCH, M., JR. and B. ANDERSON (1966) "On the balance of a set of ranks," pp. 244-268 in J. Berger, M. Zelditch, and B. Anderson (eds.) Sociological Theories in Progress, Volume I. Boston: Houghton Mifflin.

––– (1964) "Rank equilibration and political behavior." European Journal of Sociology 5, 1: 112-125.

ZIMMERMAN, W. (1972) "Hierarchical regional systems and the politics of system boundaries." International Organization 26, 1: 18-36.

ZINNES, D. A. (1970) "Coalition theories and the balance of power," in S. Groennings, E. W. Kelley, and M. Leiserson (eds.) The Study of Coalition Behavior: Theoretical Perspectives. New York: Holt, Rinehart and Winston.

––– (1967) "An analytic study of the balance of power theories." Journal of Peace Research 3: 270-288.

ZIPF, S. G. (1960) "Resistance and conformity under reward and punishment." Journal of Abnormal and Social Psychology 61, 1: 102-109.

Appendix

Table A. Major Power Totals (Actor)

	England	France	Germany	Austria	Russia	Total
Number of events initiated by each power, 1870-1881	295	149	458	280	373	1,555
Percentage of total events initiated by each power	18.9%	9.5%	29.5%	18%	24%	

Table B. Major Power Totals (Target)

	England	France	Germany	Austria	Russia	Total
Number of actions received by each power	267	246	330	318	394	1,555
Percentage of actions received by each power	17.1%	15.8%	21.2%	20.4%	25.3%	

Table C. Diplomatic Representation

	England	France	Germany	Austria	Russia
Total[a]	32	21	22	60	43
Rank Overall	3	1	2	5	4

[a] Summation of yearly rankings with 12 the best score and 60 the worst possible score.

Table D. Diplomatic Recognitions

	England	France	Germany	Austria	Russia
Total[a]	24	19	29	33	60
Rank Overall	2	1	3	4	5

[a] Summation of yearly rankings with 12 the best score and 60 the worst possible score.

Table E. Balance of Cooperation (Cooperation
Received Minus Cooperation Given)
Measured by Country for the Entire Period

	Major Power Balance of Cooperation	Systemic Balance of Cooperation
England	+6.52	+4.54
France	-33.49	-7.59
Germany	+26.39	+37.20
Austria	+21.07	+37.04
Russia	-9.07	+2.78

Table F. Direct Totals

Target

Actor	England	France	Germany	Austria	Russia
England		55.686 / 2	50.785 / 3	56.413 / 1	47.759 / 4
France	57.129 / 1		52.512 / 3	57.013 / 2	52.126 / 4
Germany	55.463 / 3	46.037 / 4		57.119 / 1	55.838 / 2
Austria	52.801 / 4	54.619 / 2	58.231 / 1		54.608 / 3
Russia	55.424 / 4	54.541 / 3	53.560 / 2	59.071 / 1	
	12	11	9	5	13

Rank order of
most direct
cooperation
received by
a nation   4   3   2   1   5

RICHARD ROSECRANCE is Carpenter Professor of International and Comparative Politics at Cornell University. He received his B.A. from Swarthmore College (1952) and his M.A. and Ph.D. from Harvard University (1957). Application of international theory to diplomatic historical periods comprises his primary field of interest, and he recently published International Relations: Peace or War? with McGraw-Hill (1973).

ALAN ALEXANDROFF is currently a Research Associate of the Situational Analysis Project at Cornell, where he is a Ph.D. Candidate in Government. He has done research in diplomatic history at the London School of Economics, and is interested in European diplomatic history and the degree to which it supports or contradicts international theory.

BRIAN HEALY, an Assistant Professor of Political Science at the University of Pennsylvania, received his M.A. from Columbia and his Ph.D. from Cornell University (1973). His fields of interest and concentration include international monetary problems and the structure of the international system. He co-authored (with Arthur Stein) "The Balance of Power in International History: Theories in Search of Reality," in the March 1973 issue of The Journal of Conflict Resolution.

ARTHUR STEIN, a Ph.D. Candidate at Yale University, received his B.A. from Cornell University. His primary field concerns the application of structural balance theory to international processes. He is co-author (with Brian Healy) of the article "The Balance of Power in International History: Theories in Search of Reality" published in the March 1973 issue of The Journal of Conflict Resolution.